The Economics of Law
An Introductory Text

CENTO VELJANOVSKI

*Research & Editorial Director,
Institute of Economic Affairs*

IEA

Published by
THE INSTITUTE OF ECONOMIC AFFAIRS
1990

First published in July 1990

by

THE INSTITUTE OF ECONOMIC AFFAIRS

2 Lord North Street, Westminster,
London SW1P 3LB

Hobart Paper 114

ISSN 0073-2818
ISBN 0-255 36227-7

The Institute gratefully acknowledges financial support for its publications programme and other work from a generous benefaction by the late Alec and Beryl Warren.

Printed in Great Britain by
GORON PRO-PRINT CO LTD
6 Marlborough Road, Churchill Industrial Estate, Lancing, W. Sussex
Text set in Berthold Baskerville

CONTENTS

[3]

[4]

FOREWORD

It is perhaps inevitable that economic thinking in the United States should often be demonstrably more advanced than in the United Kingdom.

This seems to be especially the case in the study of the combined discipline of law-and-economics. In much the same way that public choice theory had embedded itself in US economic thinking but made a lesser impact on this side of the Atlantic, law-and-economics, with its particular relevance to regulatory issues and to the application of economic analysis and insight to incentive structures within government, remains sadly under-appreciated in Britain, among academics and practitioners in both its constituent parts.

Why should this be of concern? In the first place, because it is a symptom of a more general reluctance of British economists to look at political economy in the round. As Samuel Brittan suggested in introducing the Institute's recent survey of a thousand British economists,[1] this narrowness of vision may well lead to economists being crowded out of exciting new areas by members of other disciplines—to the long-term disadvantage of the economics profession.

More important is the risk that failure to harness the rich resources of the conjoined study of law-and-economics will deprive British academics, practitioners and policy-makers of a useful tool with which to address a significant change in the nature of government activity in economic life. Over the next decade, it looks unlikely that government *ownership* of trading businesses in the productive economy will be an increasing problem, at home or abroad. Yet government *regulation* of private economic activity increases apace—from the best of motives, and as an apparently flexible tool with which to tackle a multiplicity of problems, from environmental pollution to malpractice within financial service markets.

As a result, power in Britain is shifting into the hands of regulators: at the Office of Fair Trading, the Monopolies &

[1] Martin Ricketts and Edward Shoesmith, *British Economic Opinion: A Survey of a Thousand Economists*, Research Monograph 45, London: Institute of Economic Affairs, 1990.

Mergers Commission, in OFTEL, OFGAS, OFFER and a host of 'self-regulatory' agencies operating under a statutory framework. Lawyers are heavily involved in their work, as are a smaller number of economists. What is missing is any well-developed combined intellectual framework. It would set their activities within their proper bounds, measure the costs of regulatory solutions on a consistent basis and introduce a full range of market alternatives to traditional regulatory approaches, with their heavy reliance on judgement and administrative discretion as against specific and enforceable rights measured against clear rules.

This *Hobart Paper* explores the scope to 'privatise' some of the regulatory processes. Cento Veljanovski suggests that they may be converted into more sharply defined legal rights, and that by testing them against alternatives—including insurance, or better defined penalties payable to those wronged—more effective redress may be given to those damaged, with fewer bureaucratic controls, fewer direct costs, and fewer compliance costs— frequently the most serious aspects of regulatory intervention.

Outside the formal regulatory framework, the combination of law-and-economics can be a powerful protector of individual rights. Cento Veljanovski devotes careful attention in this *Hobart Paper* to accident compensation, and shows that there may be areas where a judicial lack of familiarity with economic techniques may operate to the serious disadvantage of victims. Dr Veljanovski puts litigation in its proper perspective: as an effective means of enforcing rights. Seen in this way, Britain may be under-litigious, and abuses of power may be going unchecked because of insufficent resort to law, and in particular to law closely informed by economics.

This *Hobart Paper* appears at a particularly timely moment. In the post-Communist economies of Eastern Europe, law-and-economics is beginning spontaneously to come to the fore, as those responsible for reshaping the economic and political infrastructure of their societies come to appreciate that it is around well-defined and protected rights that their freedom and economic well-being alike depend. As ever, this *Hobart Paper* and its suggestions for new approaches reflects the views of its author, not those of the Institute, its Trustees, or Advisers. I believe that it will make an important contribution to the development of law-and-economics in Britain.

July 1990   GRAHAM MATHER

[8]

THE AUTHOR

CENTO VELJANOVSKI joined the IEA as Research & Editorial Director in January 1988. Prior to that he was in private practice; Lecturer in Law & Economics, University College, London (1984-87), and Junior Research Fellow, Centre for Socio-Legal Studies, Oxford (1978-84). He has held visiting posts at a number of North American universities and worked for a short period after graduation with the Australian Treasury. He was educated in Australia and the UK, holding several degrees in law and economics (B.Ec., M.Ec., D.Phil.). He has advised government and industry on privatisation, regulation and the media.

Dr Veljanovski is one of the few exponents of the economics of law and was the first economist appointed to a law lectureship in the UK at the University of London. He has written widely on the subject, including several books: *The New Law and Economics* (1983); (with A. S. Ogus) *Readings in the Economics of Law and Regulation* (1984); and more than a dozen articles in scholarly journals, including the *Modern Law Review* and the *Economic Journal*. He is the author of *Selling the State – Privatisation in Britain* (1987), (with W. Bishop) *Choice by Cable* (Hobart Paper 96, 1983), and most recently edited and contributed to *Privatisation and Competition: A Market Prospectus* (Hobart Paperback 28, 1989), and *Freedom in Broadcasting* (Hobart Paperback 29, 1989). He is a member of the editorial boards of the *International Review of Law and Economics*, *Law and Policy*, and the *Journal des Economistes et des Etudes Humaines*, and the advisory committees of the Erasmus Programme in Law and Economics, and Center for the Study of the New Institutional Economics (W. Germany). He was a founder member of the European Association of Law and Economics.

ACKNOWLEDGEMENTS

An early draft of this *Hobart Paper* was originally written for the IEA's conference on 'Law and Economics', which was held at the Queen Elizabeth II Conference Centre on 17 May 1989. In re-writing it for publication I am indebted to Bill Bishop, John Burton, Ralph Harris, Graham Mather, Anthony Ogus and Arthur Seldon for their comments on an earlier draft.

C.V.

I. INTRODUCTION

Increasingly, economics is being extended beyond its traditional precincts of the market-place and the economy to sociology, political science, philosophy and law. One endeavour which is gaining momentum and respectability is the economic analysis of law. This development is yet another example of the phenomenon Kenneth Boulding has called economic imperialism: 'the attempt on the part of economics to take over the other social sciences'.[1]

Most of this interest in the economic analysis of law has been shown not by economists but by lawyers mainly in North America. 'Conversational literacy in neo-classical welfare economics', observes Coleman, 'is an apparent prerequisite to gainful employment in American law schools'.[2] While this overstates the situation, it nonetheless indicates the importance that the subject has attained in North America.

In marked contrast, the study of the law in the UK is exceptionally narrow. 'The English lawyer', Ogus and Richardson comment, 'has been notoriously unwilling to admit the relevance of social science to his discipline.'[3] Similarly, UK economists have seriously lagged behind their North American counterparts. Campbell and Wiles conclude in their survey:

'in comparison with the position in America, economists in Britain have virtually ignored studies of law or the relevance of legal regulation to economic development'.[4]

'A Harmful Disciplinary Divide'

There exists an unnecessary and positively harmful disciplinary divide between law and economics which has practical conse-

[1] K. E. Boulding, 'Economics as a Moral Science', *American Economic Review*, Vol. 58, 1968, p. 8.

[2] J. L. Coleman, 'Efficiency, Exchange and Auction: Philosophical Aspects of the Economic Approach to Law', *California Law Review*, Vol. 68, 1980, p. 227.

[3] A. J. Ogus and G. Richardson, 'Economics and the Environment: A Study of Private Nuisance', *Cambridge Law Journal*, Vol. 26, 1977, pp. 284-325.

[4] C. Campbell and P. Wiles, 'The Study of Law in Society', *Law and Society Review*, Vol. 10, 1976, pp. 563-64.

BOX 1

'A Deadly Combination':
Law Without Economics

'Judges move slower than markets but faster than the economics profession, a deadly combination.'
Judge F. Easterbrook (1987)

'A lawyer who has not studied economics ... is very apt to become a public enemy.' *Justice Brandeis (1916)*

'... every lawyer ought to seek an understanding of economics. There we are called on to consider and weigh the ends of legislation, the means of attaining them, and the cost. We learn that for everything we have to give up something else, and we are taught to set the advantage we gain against the other advantage we lose and to know what we are doing when we elect.'
Justice O. W. Holmes (1897)

'[Economics] is a powerful, and quite general tool of analysis that everybody who thinks and writes about law uses, consciously or not, ... it provides a convenient starting point for a general theory of law in society. It also—and this point must be stressed—has a strong empirical basis, and a basis in common sense. All about us is ample evidence that the system does use its pricing mechanism (in the broadest sense) to manipulate behaviour, and pervasively.'
Professor L. Friedman (1984)

'For the rational study of the law, the black letterman may be the man of the present, but the man of the future is the man of statistics and the master of economics.'
Justice O. W. Holmes (1897)

quences. Both disciplines suffer from what Veblen called 'trained incapacity'. Lawyers and policy-makers are economically illiterate and frequently innumerate. The English legal fraternity is wary of theory, contemptuous of experts and academics, and reluctant to accept the idea that other disciplines have something valuable to say about 'law'. The situation is precisely captured by Professor Patrick Atiyah:

'Most English judges are emphatically neither intellectuals nor theorists; few are ever given to doubting their own first principles, at least in public, and most are deeply sceptical of the value of theory. ... Very few have more than the faintest glimmering of the vast jurisprudential literature concerning the nature of the judicial process. Most would pride themselves on being pragmatists, and not theorists.'[1]

To the economist, the approach of lawyers is excessively descriptive and legalistic. On the occasions that they do venture to comment on legal reform, their conclusions appear *ad hoc* rationalisations, ethical and moralistic value-judgements, or simply assertions based on dubious casual empiricism. The economics editor of the Australian *Sydney Morning Herald* captured the lawyers' approach in his blunt attack on a proposal by the Law Reform Commission to permit class actions as:

'... a highly interventionist remedy, typical of the legal mind. It ignores many of the economic issues involved and falls back on the lawyer's conviction that all of the world's problems can be solved if only we had the right laws. Finding a lawyer who understands and respects market forces is as hard as finding a baby-wear manufacturer who understands and respects celibacy. *The legally trained mind cannot grasp that it is never possible to defeat market forces, only to distort them so they pop up in unexpected ways.*'[2]

Economists, too, must shoulder considerable criticism. The general inclination, particularly, though not exclusively, of British economists, is to treat the law as datum. Professor Karl Llewellyn touched on this many years ago in a comment which still accurately describes the attitude of most economists:

'... the economist takes ... [the law] for granted. Law exists. If it serves economic life well, he has ignored it; if ill, he has pithily cursed it and its devotees, without too great an effort to understand the reason of disservice'.[3]

This is now changing. In the academic climate of the 1970s it was difficult to present economic views of law principally because the idea appeared irrelevant, seen as largely imported from the United States where market and free-enterprise values are more acceptable and accepted. The 1980s has seen free-market economic thinking move to the centre of government

[1] P. S. Atiyah, 'The Legacy of Holmes Through English Eyes', *Boston University Law Review*, Vol. 63, 1983, p. 380.

[2] *Sydney Morning Herald*, 25 May 1981.

[3] K. N. Llewellyn, 'The Effect of Legal Institutions Upon Economics', *American Economic Review*, Vol. 136, 1925, p. 665.

[13]

policy in Europe and many other parts of the world. The supply-side policies of the Thatcher Government have given an intellectual impetus to the economic analysis of laws and regulation. Privatisation and the regulation of utility industries, such as gas, water, and electricity, have brought into prominence the economic dimension of different laws. But even though economics has, and will increasingly, become central to the control of industry as we move from nationalisation to regulation, the basis of the new regulatory approach has not exhibited a deep concern for sound economic principles. In the UK the rhetoric of economic rationalism may have been adopted to justify the growth of regulation, but the reality is an *ad hoc* assembly of laws and decisions cemented together by the greatest of all expedients—political compromise implemented through bureaucratic discretion.

'Economics of Law'

In this *Hobart Paper* I shall explore how economics has been, and can be, used to analyse law—a new sphere of study known as the 'economics of law'.

The economics of law can be defined rather crudely as the application of economic theory, mostly price theory, and statistical methods to examine the formation, structure, processes and impact of the law and legal institutions. It consists of a dispersed and unsystematic literature written by economists and lawyers. No consensus has yet emerged, nor do economists possess a coherent explanatory theory of law. Nevertheless, in the last decade it has developed into a distinct field of study with its own specialist scholars, journals[1] and texts,[2] with every indication that interest in the field is growing.

The economics of law is not confined to those areas of law that directly affect markets or economic activity. It goes well beyond these areas to examine fundamental legal institutions. The subject can be arbitrarily separated into 'old' and 'new' parts. The old law-and-economics is concerned with laws that affect the operation of the economy and markets. It examines the effects the law has on competition, the performance of markets, industries and firms, and economic variables such as prices, investment, profits, income distribution and resource allocation

---

[1] Most notably, *The Journal of Law & Economics*, *The Journal of Legal Studies*, *International Review of Law and Economics*, and *Journal of Law, Economics and Organization*.

[2] See 'Select Bibliography', below, pp. 91-95.

generally. It includes competition law, industry regulation (the regulation of the privatised utilities and nationalised industries, quotas and price controls), and tax and trade laws. This application is witnessing a resurgence in the UK and Europe as the supply-side reforms of privatisation and liberalisation para- doxically thrust government regulation of industry to the forefront.

The most innovative extension of economics in recent years has been the 'new' law-and-economics which takes as its subject- matter the entire legal and regulatory systems irrespective of whether or not the law controls economic relationships. In recent years contract, tort (the area of the common law which deals with unintentional harms such as accidents and nuisance), family law, criminal law and legal procedure have all been subjected to economic analysis. This area of study is most associated with the work of Judge Richard A. Posner when a Professor of Law at the University of Chicago. His text, *Economic Analysis of Law*, now in its third edition, illustrates the rich variety of legal topics which can be analysed using economics.

Law as a 'Giant Pricing Machine'

In this *Hobart Paper* I begin by outlining very briefly the nature and history of the economics of law. This has been principally a North American development, and one in which lawyers, or those trained in both law *and* economics, have contributed most. In Section III the differences between economic and legal reasoning are discussed at length. The defining concepts of economics are choice, the principle of substitutability at the margin, opportunity costs, and allocative efficiency. Yet non- economists, particularly lawyers, regard economics as a subject confined to material wealth and financial considerations. This misconception has led to needless confusion and an artificial barrier to the acceptance of economics among lawyers and as a basis for legal reform. The major difference between lawyers and economists is that the latter see law as a 'giant pricing machine'— laws act as prices or taxes which provide incentives. It is this perspective which marks out the economist's contribution to legal analysis. Section IV examines in more detail the way economists approach the legal system. Sections V and VI supply some examples of the differing applications of economics to tort, criminal law, legal doctrines and regulation.

II. SHORT HISTORY

The marrying of economics and law is not new. 'Economic' approaches to law can be found in the utilitarianism of Beccaria-Bonesara (1764)[1] and Jeremy Bentham (1789);[2] the political economy of Adam Smith (1776)[3] and Karl Marx (1861);[4] and the American Institutionalist school, most notably in the work of John R. Commons (1929).[5] Indeed, a strong case can be made that the genesis of economics as a subject in its own right grew out of the moral and political philosophy of Adam Smith, the founder of modern economics. Smith's *Wealth of Nations* was only one part of a more general theory embracing law. His *Lectures on Jurisprudence* were, unfortunately, never completed. Yet the connections between law and economics appear to lie in the origins of economics itself. Indeed, they are perhaps even genetically related, for Smith's father—who died before his son's birth—was Clerk to the Court Martial and Comptroller of Customs, Kirkaldy, and Adam himself was a Commissioner for Customs.[6] Thus the idea of an economic approach to law is not a novel one; it has simply been neglected to the detriment of both subjects. Indeed, Anglo-American common law has been profoundly affected by economics, especially the law of contract and tort.

Disciplinary Divides

Despite this pedigree, during the period 1920-60 the economic study of law and institutions fell into disrepute among Anglo-American economists. An active interaction between the two continued in the USA where the law had economic objectives and/or effects, as in competition law, and in the regulation of

---

[1] Beccaria-Bonesara, *An Essay in Crime and Punishment* (1764), New York: Oceania Publishers, 1958.

[2] J. Bentham, *An Introduction to the Principles of Morals and Legislation*, 1789.

[3] Adam Smith, *The Wealth of Nations*, 1776.

[4] Karl Marx, *Das Kapital*, 1861.

[5] J. R. Commons, *Legal Foundations of Capitalism*, New York: Macmillan, 1924.

[6] I am indebted to Professor John Burton for drawing this interesting information to my attention.

[16]

public utility industries such as gas and railroads. But in the UK, largely because of nationalisation and the moribund state of its competition laws, little work was undertaken even on these subjects.[1]

The neglect of institutions among economists can be attributed to two factors. First, many North American economists associated the study of law and organisations with the Institutionalists such as John R. Commons, whose work they regarded as legalistic and lacking in rigour. Thus in 1959 Henry Houthakker, a respected economist, was able to write:

'The economic analysis of institutions is not highly regarded or widely practised among contemporary economists. The very word "institution" now carries unfavourable associations with the legalistic approach to economic phenomena that was respectable during the first three decades of this century. There is little reason to regret the triumphant reaction that swept institutionalism from its dominant place. Nevertheless, economics can still learn much from the study of institutions. The analytical problems that arise are often both a challenge to conventional theory and a useful reminder of the relativity of accepted doctrine.'[2]

Professor Mark Blaug suggests that the core of Institutionalism was a dissatisfaction with the high level of abstraction of neo-classical economics. The institutionalists called for the integration of economics with the other social sciences and for more empirical study.[3] Institutionalism has not survived, being regarded by many as no more than a useful set of criticisms of mainstream economics.

The second reason for this neglect lies in the transformation of economics from an *a priori* to an empirical science. The growing influence of positivism in economics, coupled with the increasing use of mathematics[4] and statistical analysis, directed the economist's attention to areas of research where 'hard' data could be found. Institutions and law appeared to defy either

[1] R. B. Stevens and B. S. Yamey, *The Restrictive Trade Practices Court*, London: Weidenfeld & Nicolson, 1965.

[2] H. S. Houthakker, 'The Scope and Limits of Futures Trading', in M. Abramovitz *et al.* (eds.), *Allocation of Economic Resources*, California: Stanford University Press, 1959, p. 134.

[3] M. Blaug, *Economic Theory in Retrospect*, London: Heinemann, 2nd edn., 1970, pp. 678-79.

[4] This can effectively be dated from Samuelson's classic article on public goods ('The Pure Theory of Public Expenditure', *Review of Economics and Statistics*, Vol. 36, 1954, pp. 387-89) which illustrated in three pages the power of mathematics to express a concept that had eluded economists.

mathematical modelling or easy empirical analysis, and were therefore ignored. This remains the case for the bulk of economics today. A perusal of the leading professional journals will leave the reader with the impression that economics is a branch of applied mathematics, far removed from the everyday economic difficulties that face ordinary citizens. Economics has become a mathematical fantasia where the honours go to those versed in calculus, topology, set theory, linear algebra and the like. 'Page after page of the professional economic journals', observes Wassily Leontief, a Nobel prizewinner in economics, 'are filled with mathematical formulae leading to precisely stated but irrelevant conclusions.'[1] This view is shared by one of the greatest of contemporary institutional economists, Professor Ronald Coase: 'In my youth it was said what was too silly to be said may be sung. In modern economics it may be put into mathematics.'[2] There is a hope harboured by some that the growth of the economics of law will eventually lead to a reversal of this trend and a renaissance of political economy.

Among lawyers the reluctance to engage in interdisciplinary teaching and research stems from a number of factors. The first is the influence exerted by practitioners on legal education. Law, unlike economics, is a profession. A law degree is a professional qualification primarily designed to equip the student for practice, and hence legal education in the UK and most other English-language countries must train the lawyer to ply his or her trade. Indeed, before the Second World War many English university law courses were taught by part-time practising lawyers. The subservience of the study of law to the demands of the practising profession in the UK has placed severe limitations on the ability of legal education to explore the wider context of the law, and has bred a hostility to attempts to broaden the base of legal education. Secondly, legal education, particularly the case method which requires students to study hundreds of cases, is not conducive to the ready acceptance of the social science approach which seeks to identify generalities rather than the peculiarities of situations which fascinate the legal mind.

[1] *The Economist*, 17 July 1982.

[2] R. H. Coase, *The Firm, the Market and the Law*, Chicago: University of Chicago Press, 1988.

Resurgence of Legal Economics

The growing interest in law-and-economics is intimately associated with, although by no means confined to,[1] the writings of members of the law and economics faculties of the University of Chicago.

The 'Chicago School's' analysis of law and institutions is hard to define in any specific way. Most would, however, agree that its hallmark is the belief that simple market economics has extraordinary explanatory power in all fields of human and institutional activity. It applies the simple tenets of rational maximising behaviour to all walks of life to elicit testable propositions about the way people and institutions will react to changes in their environment, and to construct proposals for legal reform based on the criterion of economic efficiency.

The Chicago programme in law and economics dates back to the early 1940s when Henry Simons was appointed to the law faculty. After Simons's death in 1947, Aaron Director took over his teaching responsibilities and in 1949 was appointed Professor of Economics in the Law School. Director exerted a considerable intellectual influence on the economics of anti-trust through the work of his students, such as Bowman, Bork and Manne.[2] This activity in the law-and-economics of anti-trust, coupled with the policy orientation of Chicago economists, provided the impetus for a more general economic study of law. In 1958, the law and economics programme at Chicago entered a new phase with the founding of the *Journal of Law and Economics* under the editorship first of Aaron Director and then of Ronald Coase.[3]

The subsequent development of the economic analysis of law can be divided into three phases which broadly coincide with each of the three decades of the 1960s, 1970s and 1980s.

---

[1] There are a number of approaches which for the most part differ in the emphasis they place on market behaviour and the complexity of decision-making. For a different approach, O. E. Williamson, *The Economic Institutions of Capitalism*, New York: The Free Press, 1985. See discussion in C. G. Veljanovski, *The New Law and Economics*, Oxford: Centre for Socio-Legal Studies, 1983.

[2] Two important statements of Chicago anti-trust economics are R. H. Bork, *The Antitrust Paradox – A Policy at War with Itself*, New York: Basic Books, 1978; R. A. Posner, *Antitrust Law – An Economic Perspective*, Chicago: University of Chicago Press, 1976.

[3] For an account of the law-and-economics programme at Chicago prior to 1960, E. Kitch (ed.), 'The Fire of Truth: A Remembrance of Law and Economics at Chicago, 1932-1970', *Journal of Law and Economics*, Vol. 26, 1983, pp. 163-234.

The Sixties – Utility Regulation and Accidents

The 1960s represent the formative stages of the law-and-economics movement. The increasing importance of government intervention in the US economy led some economists to devote attention to modelling and measuring the effects of regulation on industry. The classic articles by Averch and Johnson,[1] Caves,[2] and Stigler and Friedland[3] mark the beginning of the rigorous attempts by economists to model so-called public utility regulation. Another landmark was Alfred Kahn's *The Economics of Regulation*, published in two volumes in 1970 and 1971.[4] In a different way the Chicago economist, Professor George Stigler,[5] set out the rudiments of a positive theory of regulation which indicated that governments were unlikely to be interested in efficiency or some broadly defined concept of the public interest. His central hypothesis was that regulation is secured by politically effective interest groups, invariably producers or sections of the regulated industry, rather than consumers. 'As a rule', argues Stigler, 'regulation is acquired by industry and is designed and operated primarily for its benefit' by redistributing income in favour of the regulated industry in return for electoral support for politicians who engineer the redistribution. This view of regulation has now gained wide acceptance from the political Left and Right. It underpins the Thatcher Government's attempts to lift the burden of government red-tape from industry. A large number of regulations are seen as barriers to competition, thus impairing the wealth-creating process. The prime movers of the growth of regulation during the 1960s and 1970s are seen as industry itself:

> 'Corporatism limited competition and the birth of new firms whilst, at the same time, encouraging protectionism and restrictions designed to help existing firms.'[6]

[1] H. Averch and L. Johnson, 'Behavior of the Firm under Regulatory Constraint', *American Economic Review*, Vol. LII, 1962, pp. 1,052-69.

[2] R. Caves, *Air Transport and its Regulators: An Industry Study*, Cambridge, Mass.: Harvard University Press, 1962.

[3] G. J. Stigler and C. Friedland, 'What Can Regulators Regulate?: The Case of Electricity', *Journal of Law and Economics*, Vol. 5, 1962, pp. 1-16.

[4] This work has since been reprinted as one volume: A. E. Kahn, *The Economics of Regulation: Principles and Institutions*, Cambridge, Mass.: MIT Press, 1988.

[5] G. J. Stigler, 'The Theory of Economic Regulation', *Bell Journal of Economics and Management Science*, Vol. 2, 1971, pp. 3-21. For a sample of subsequent 'Chicago' research, G. J. Stigler (ed.), *Chicago Studies in Political Economy*, Chicago: University of Chicago Press, 1988.

[6] DTI, *Enterprise*, Cm. 278, London: HMSO, 1988, para. 1.3.

Stigler's hypothesis, together with work in the area of public utilities, stimulated economists in the 1970s to undertake empirical studies of the effects of regulation on industrial performance.[1]

Calabresi's Theory of Accident Liability

Two other studies during the 1960s stand out as highly influential. Both were about tort law—the common law governing the liability of injurers for damages—and graphically different from the work on regulation. The seminal study by Professor Guido Calabresi (of Yale University), 'Some Thoughts on Risk Distribution and the Law of Torts',[2] was the first systematic attempt by a lawyer to examine the law of torts from an economic perspective. Calabresi argued that the goal of accident law was to 'minimise the sum of the costs of accidents and the costs of preventing accidents'. He later refined this axiom into a theory of liability for accident losses. According to Calabresi, the costs of accidents could be minimised if the party which could avoid the accident at least-cost was made liable for the loss. This Calabresi called the 'cheapest-cost-avoider' rule.[3] His idea is simple to illustrate. A careless driver's car collides with a pedestrian, inflicting damages totalling £200. It is discovered that the accident resulted from the driver's failure to fit new brakes costing £50. Clearly, road users and society as a whole would benefit if the driver had fitted new brakes, the benefit being £150 (equal to the avoided loss of £200 minus the cost of the new brakes, £50). If the driver is made legally liable for the loss, that is, he is required to pay the victim compensation of £200 should an accident occur, then clearly he would have a strong incentive to fit the new brakes. A liability rule which shifts the loss whenever it would encourage careless drivers to fit new brakes makes the cheapest solution to the individual the efficient solution.

The distinctive quality of Calabresi's work was to show the power of simple economic principles to rationalise a whole body of law, and to develop a coherent basis for its reform.

---

[1] For an assessment of this theory by one of its adherents, S. Peltzman, 'The Economic Theory of Regulation after a Decade of Deregulation', in *Brookings Papers on Economic Activity—Microeconomics*, Washington DC: Brookings Institution, 1989.

[2] *Yale Law Journal*, Vol. 70, 1967, pp. 499-553.

[3] G. Calabresi, *The Costs of Accidents: A Legal and Economic Analysis*, New Haven: Yale University Press, 1970.

The Coase Theorem

The second, and more important, article was Ronald Coase's 'The Problem of Social Costs'.[1] This had a profound effect on the economic approach to law and remains a source of lively controversy. 'Social Costs' develops many themes, yet its primary purpose was to correct what was, in Coase's view, a fundamental misconception in the way economists approached questions of policy.

Economists generally give policy advice on the basis of the concept of market failure.[2] Typically, a departure from a model of a perfectly competitive market constitutes a *prima facie* case for government intervention. Economists treated government as a costless corrective force. They had in effect created an unfounded dichotomy between an imperfect market and perfect government.

Coase argued that realistic policy could be devised only if each situation was subjected to detailed investigation based on comparing the total costs and benefits of actual and proposed policy alternatives. Both the market and the non-market solutions were costly, and these had to be dealt with on an equal footing when deciding which policy to pursue.[3] This is not what economists habitually did, nor do many do so now (see Section VI).

Coase's article is famous for another reason. As a basis for the analysis of the English common law of nuisance (as, for example, pollution), Coase elaborated a proposition which later became known as the 'Coase Theorem'. The Theorem holds that in a world where bargaining is costless, property rights will be transferred to those who value them the highest. Moreover, Coase argued that the level of pollution would be the same whether the law held the polluter liable for the damages or not, provided that the parties could get together to bargain relatively cheaply. The only impact of the law may be on the relative wealth of individuals. That is, potential gains-from-trade—and not the law—would determine the allocation of resources. This counter-intuitive conclusion and its implication for policy analysis is explained in more detail in Section III.

[1] *Journal of Law and Economics*, Vol. 3, 1960, pp. 1-44.

[2] T. Cowen (ed.), *The Theory of Market Failure—A Critical Examination*, Fairfax: George Mason University Press, 1988.

[3] C. Wolf, Jr., *Markets or Government—Choosing between Imperfect Alternatives*, Cambridge, Mass.: MIT Press, 1988.

In other areas of economics, developments were taking place which gradually combined to give institutional considerations greater emphasis in the way some prominent economists began to think about the economy.

The Economic Approach to Non-Market Behaviour

In the 1960s a small number of economists studying fiscal policy began to question the relevance of orthodox economics. The 'market failure' approach simply did not yield policy proposals that governments followed, nor did it explain the behaviour of bureaucrats and politicians. In the early 1960s, a handful of economists, drawing on the work of earlier continental economists such as Wicksell, Lindahl and others, began to incorporate government and bureaucracy into their models. They, like Coase, emphasised that the relevant comparison was not between ideals but between feasible, imperfect and costly alternatives; they therefore started to develop a 'government failure' framework comparable to that of market failure.

Public Choice (or the 'Economics of Politics') made governmental behaviour subject to the same self-regarding forces as those found in markets. Beginning with Downs's *An Economic Theory of Democracy*[1] and Buchanan and Tullock's *The Calculus of Consent*,[2] economists began to explain political and bureaucratic behaviour by building on the economic postulate that politicians and civil servants as a class are principally motivated by self-interest. The economics of politics seeks to develop models of social behaviour that do not differ in fundamental respects from those applied to individual actions in the market-place.[3]

In 1957 Gary Becker published his doctoral dissertation on the economics of sex and racial discrimination in labour markets, which had hitherto been seen as exclusively a social problem.[4] This work began a career devoted to applying economics to a wide variety of non-market behaviour such as

[1] New York: Harper and Row, 1957.

[2] Ann Arbor: University of Michigan Press, 1962.

[3] G. Tullock, *The Vote Motive*, Hobart Paperback No. 9, London: IEA, 1976. A closely aligned field of study is 'rent-seeking': C. K. Rowley, R. D. Tollison and G. Tullock (eds.), *The Political Economy of Rent-Seeking*, Boston: Kluwer Academic Publishers, 1988.

[4] G. S. Becker, *The Economics of Discrimination*, Chicago: University of Chicago Press, 1957.

[23]

crime, politics, education, the family, health and charity.[1] Becker unashamedly extended the utility maximisation hypothesis to all individual choices, whether they occurred in the market or not. The scope of economics as a science was seen as coterminous with the study of choice—a problem that pervades all human activity. Becker's work demonstrated that non-market behaviour could be modelled rigorously, and in this way legitimised amongst economists the study of issues normally considered the province of other social scientists.

The early work on property rights by Alchian[2] and Demsetz[3] added an explicit institutional dimension to the extension of economics. As already noted, economic theory operates in an institutional vacuum, focussing on the production, distribution and consumption of physical goods and services. Property rights theorists stress that the value of goods and services depends crucially on the 'bundle of legal rights' transferred with them, and that markets trade in these legal rights. Economics is, in effect, the study of how variations in 'bundles of property rights' affect prices and the allocation of resources. Clearly, the price of a freehold property differs from that of a leasehold or tenancy, and these different forms of ownership rights affect the efficiency with which land is used.[4]

An Arcane Pursuit

In this the formative decade, the economic analysis of law was regarded for the most part as a peripheral and somewhat arcane pursuit. With the notable exception of Calabresi, it was almost entirely the province of economists. The literature of this period concerned itself with the economic analysis of the impact of government regulations (such as minimum wage laws, competition and public utility policies) on the market-place, and a

[1] G. S. Becker, *The Economic Approach to Human Behaviour*, Chicago: University of Chicago Press, 1976; G. S. Becker and W. M. Landes (eds.), *Essays in the Economics of Crime and Punishment*, New York: Columbia University Press, 1974; G. S. Becker, *A Treatise on the Family*, Cambridge, Mass.: Harvard University Press, 1981.

[2] A. A. Alchian, *Some Economics of Property Rights*, Santa Monica: Rand Paper No. 2,316, 1961; *Pricing and Society*, Occasional Paper No. 17, London: IEA, 1967.

[3] H. Demsetz, 'Some Aspects of Property Rights', *Journal of Law and Economics*, Vol. 9, 1964, pp. 61-70; 'Toward a Theory of Property Rights', *American Economic Review*, Vol. 59, 1969, pp. 347-59.

[4] See J. Burton in S. N. S. Cheung, *The Myth of Social Cost*, Hobart Paper 82, London: IEA, 1978.

running debate, still unresolved, over the validity and implications of Coase's analysis.

In the UK the subject was all but ignored. A few isolated economists became intrigued by it, but there was very little scope for serious research because the UK's legal and political structures were very different from those in North America. The USA, with 51 state/federal jurisdictions, provides lawyers and economists with a rich laboratory to evaluate laws critically— something which is absent in the UK. Nonetheless, in 1970 Professor Patrick Atiyah published *Accidents, Compensation and the Law*,[1] which introduced the British reader to Calabresi's economics, igniting interest among lawyers in the reform of the tort system and the efficiency of accident compensation schemes.

The 1970s: Posner's Efficiency Analysis

The 1970s can be described as the growth decade of the law-and-economics movement. Increasingly, North American legal scholars began to use economics to rationalise and appraise the law, and by the end of the decade the law-and-economics movement had firmly established itself as a respectable component of legal studies. In the area of regulation a growing number of studies challenged the belief that regulation was effective.

If one personality had to be chosen to represent this period, it would be Professor (now Judge) Richard Posner of the University of Chicago Law School (now of the US Court of Appeals).[2] Although Posner's work remains controversial, there is no doubt that his contributions are both important and durable.

Posner demonstrated that simple economic concepts could be used to analyse all areas of law—contract, property, criminal, family, commercial, constitutional, administrative and procedural law. His treatise, *Economic Analysis of Law*, is a *tour de force* of subtle and detailed applications of economics to law. He has shown that the doctrines and procedural rules of legal systems can be given economic explanation and rationalisation. This type of economic analysis of law (which is discussed further in Section IV) attempts to explain the nature of legal doctrines

---

[1] London: Weidenfeld & Nicolson, 1970.

[2] R. A. Posner, *Economic Analysis of Law*, Boston: Little Brown, 3rd edn., 1988; *The Economics of Justice*, Boston: Harvard University Press, 1981; W. M. Landes and R. A. Posner, *The Economic Structure of Tort Law*, Cambridge, Mass.: Harvard University Press, 1988.

using the concept of economic efficiency. While this approach is fraught with difficulties, Posner's work, beginning with his paper, 'A Theory of Negligence',[1] and refined in an impressive sequence of articles and books, ushered in a new branch of economic analysis of law, one that the lawyer could use to discover the basis of the hotchpotch of doctrines which make up the common law.

Posner rose to prominence, even notoriety, and captured the imagination of a generation of scholars by going further to advance the radical thesis that the fundamental logic of the common law was economic. He argued that judges unwittingly decided cases in a way that encouraged a more efficient allocation of resources.

To the economist, this claim is remarkable for two reasons—judges typically reject economic arguments and, when they do employ economics, it is invariably wrongly applied. Moreover, Posner argued that economics could 'explain' legal doctrines even though these doctrines purported to have no explicit economic basis.

Law and Economics in the 1980s

The 1980s has been a period of maturation and consolidation. In the USA many of the prominent scholars in the field (Posner, Bork, Easterbrook, Scalia, and Breyer) have been elevated to the bench under President Reagan's administration, and the importance of economics—especially supply-side reforms—have been catapulted to the forefront of political and legal debates by reforming governments in both the West and the East. In the USA, Professor (now Judge) Easterbrook has claimed that:

> 'The Justices [of the US Supreme Court] are more sophisticated in economic reasoning, and they apply it in a more thoroughgoing way, than at any time in our history.'[2]

Elsewhere, policies such as privatisation, liberalisation, deregulation and *perestroika* all contain major changes in the institutions and laws governing economic activity.

In the UK, the use of economics to analyse law and regulation is just beginning to gain a toe-hold, largely due to the supply-side

---

[1] *Journal of Legal Studies*, Vol. 1, 1972, pp. 28-96.

[2] F. Easterbrook, 'Foreword: The Court and the Economic System', *Harvard Law Review*, Vol. 98, 1984, p. 45.

reforms of the Thatcher Government. The growth of regulation as a result of privatisation has drawn attention to the need to consider its economic basis—its rationale, costs, benefits and impact—if it is to be effective in achieving desired objectives with the least waste of scarce resources. What is less clearly understood is the positive theory of regulation which seeks to explain why, despite good intentions and sound analysis, governments frequently ignore efficiency and effectiveness as the governing criteria for regulatory reforms. Rather, the political market-place generates regulation which is costly and wasteful in order to satisfy pressure groups and administrative convenience. The tensions between the political and economic 'market-places' are in large part the core of economics, and the hunting ground of practitioners of the economics of law.

III. THE ECONOMIC APPROACH

It is apparent to any observer that lawyers and economists think and argue in radically different ways. Legal reasoning proceeds by example, argument and the interpretation and meaning of words. Lawyers are trained to distinguish and interpret legal opinions, identify salient facts and apply the law to those facts. Backed into a corner, the lawyer, the judge, and most policy-makers will claim that an understanding of economics is not useful. It is confusing, they argue, because economists disagree with one another (ask two economists and you might get three opinions), reach no clear conclusion (if all the economists were placed end-to-end, they would not reach a firm conclusion), the economy is in a mess, and, in any case, the law pursues goals that in the main are not economic in character. In this and the next section the nature and tools of economic reasoning, and what distinguishes them from those of legal reasoning, are discussed.

A Biblical Parable

When God created the world he put Adam and Eve in the Garden of Eden. At more or less the same time he did two other things:

First, he laid down a 'law': don't eat the apples;

Second, he gave Adam and Eve the ability to choose.

We all know what they did. They broke the law and committed the human race to eternal damnation in a world where resources are scarce and where people are selfish. *GOD* gave man a choice—a legal choice—and man created an economic problem. Instead of an effortless paradise he is required to toil and to determine his own destiny. Thus our legal and economic systems began with the same act of law-breaking.

This biblical parable offers us several truths. First, that law and economics deal with essentially the same problems: scarcity with its conflict of interests and how to channel selfishness into socially desirable outcomes. Second, that economists have been wise to build their discipline on a model of man which assumes that he acts principally out of self-interest. On the whole, people are not saints. A legal or economic system which is built on altruism will soon collapse even if it offers people the prospect of paradise. God could not do it; no man or society has yet proved God deficient. Finally, it tells us that, even with the assistance of divine guidance, it is a mistake to believe that there is a one-to-one correspondence between what the law says and what people do. People will obey the law only if it is in their interests to do so, and they will, in any event, try to minimise the disadvantages that laws impose on them.

Economists and lawyers may not belong to the oldest profession, although they are frequently accused of behaving as if they did, but they are both concerned with resolving the oldest problem—how to reconcile individual freedoms when individual interests conflict. The market is one solution; the law another. And the two interact.

Economics, then, is about the choices that the Adams and Eves of this world make. It is the systematic study of the factors affecting choice: the advantages and disadvantages and the way these are balanced, and about the way individuals evolve social institutions to deal with scarcity and to control private interest.

Economics as the Study of Choice

Two questions naturally arise: How can economics be applied to the study of law?, and why should it be?

Economics is typically viewed as the study of inflation, unemployment and markets, subjects which seem to have only a glancing relevance to whether a negligent doctor should compensate his patient for sawing off the wrong leg, whether a newspaper should pay compensation in a libel action, or what types of safety regulation are effective. Yet the economic analysis of law uses the same economics to investigate these questions as it does to assist in analysing the price of timber or whether a restrictive contract is anti-competitive. This is known as price theory: the study of the interaction and behaviour of individual units in the economy—the firm, the consumer, the worker.

There are two reasons why this branch of economics can and is applied to law. The first is that, whether we like it or not, or whether we approve of economics or not, economic consider-ations do have a profound effect on the way the law functions in practice. Take the example of tort which, as will be shown below (pp. 63-72), governs civil liability for wrongs such as negligently

[29]

caused motor accidents. Accidents and harms are not only physical events giving rise to the possibility of legal action and medical treatment; they are also economic events. An accident consumes resources; its avoidance is costly, and the hospitalisation and medical treatment of victims is also costly. In a society where resources are scarce, rules of law are required that not only provide a just solution but one which avoids waste by reducing the costs of accidents.

There is an overwhelming tendency for lawyers and laymen to treat law as a set of rules and procedures, which can distort the perception of its impact. The law, for example, bans a certain substance or awards compensation to victims according to stated principles which provide full compensation. Reaching for legal textbooks to learn about how law affects individuals is about as much use as reading the Communist Manifesto to gain an understanding of the upheaval in communist countries. Knowledge of the law is only the first incomplete step to understanding the subject. Well over 95 per cent of tort cases, for example, are settled out of court. The reason is straightforward—settlement is cheaper than litigation. This economic factor has a profound effect on the nature of the legal system because it compromises the plaintiff's rights. There are the formal laws governing liability and compensation. But the parties through their solicitors in negotiation determine the actual level of compensation, and the costs and uncertainty of litigation ensure that the plaintiff does not receive the full amount of monetary compensation to which he is formally entitled under the law.

This procedure has two implications for the practising lawyer. First, if a lawyer has a representative case-load he can expect to act as a negotiator in well over 95 per cent of cases. Secondly, knowledge of the technical rules of the law provides very little indication of how the law is used in practice and, more importantly, its effects. It is clear that the rules and legal measure of damages will in most cases only be used as 'threats'—as upper limits to the negotiated settlement. In the negotiation process the legal rules are not only taken out of the control of the courts but compromised. The victim's lawyer quickly becomes embroiled in trading uncertainty as to liability with lower settlement sums. These are economic issues and, of course, since the typical remedy available to the successful plaintiff is financial—the award of monetary compensation—economics has a natural place in the theory and practice of the law. Even in the criminal law, justice is bargained through the 'plea bargain' which is discussed at greater length in Section V (pp. 59-62).

These considerations are not, however, the principal reasons for the intrusion of economics into legal thinking. In essence, the economics used is little more than common sense applied in a systematic way. This is because economics is the study of choice, of alternatives and objectives, and of the reconciliation between conflicting objectives. The hallmark of economic reasoning is its analysis of purposeful human and institutional behaviour, by which I mean *the analysis of rational action related to the objectives to be achieved.*

The view of many contemporary economists, and the one which lies at the root of the extension of economics to law, is that any question which involves a choice, whether it be the price to be charged by British Coal or the determination of liability by a judge, has an economic dimension. Choices also have ethical dimensions and political consequences. Thus the significance of economics is limited by the nature of the choice but not restricted to examining the obvious financial and economic consequences of the law. It is concerned with analysing the choices which individuals in their roles as judges, people at risk, litigants and lawyers make in response to harms, to the law and other factors such as costs, income, and so on.

A Theoretical Framework

The Nature of Theory

A major reason for the tension between lawyer and economist concerns the role of theory. Lawyers do not think in terms of theories. The lawyer's method of analysis is literary; it is reasoning by metaphor, analogy and simile. His empirical method is the study of past cases and statutes, common sense, introspection, anecdotes and experience. Indeed, the common law method, which has had a profound effect on legal thinking, is intensely pragmatic and inductive.

This would not be a matter for concern if the only function of those trained in law was to act as legal practitioners sifting the law reports to advise clients of their contents. But lawyers have a broader influence. They form part of our academic institutions; from their ranks come a disproportionate number of parliamentarians and individuals influential in determining policy, and they advise on, draft and propose laws. Yet their knowledge of the law does not equip them to cope adequately with the problems of legal change and reform. It would be only a slight exaggeration to say that the English legal profession is in deep crisis because of its inadequate and narrow training. Its professional standing is lower than that of accountants, and its ability to advise clients on the implication of laws for their business activities borders on the naive. It would in fact be difficult to point to any other profession which has so deliberately narrowed its market.

Law is parasitic on the social sciences, philosophy and other disciplines precisely because of its narrow intellectual base which has deprived the subject of a theoretical framework. It is, as Judge Bork has said, 'a ship with a great deal of sail but a very shallow keel'.[1] Law, according to Professor Lon Fuller,

'is the only human study having no distinctive end of its own. Where its ends can be regarded as grounded in reason, and not brute expressions of political power, those ends must be derived not from law itself but from ethics, sociology and economics'.[2]

The lawyer's best defences are attack and obscurantism. The secrets of the law, claim lawyers, will not yield to a single theory. Law is too complex and confused to be explained by any one theory; it rides many different horses at the same time. Lawyers are hostile to theory with its broad generalisations based on simplifying assumptions. The postulates of the economist seem to the lawyer fragile, narrow and technical, and to be couched in so many qualifications as to render the economist's pronouncements irrelevant; or they are stated with such sweeping generality that it is difficult to apply them to specific factual settings. Lawyers are more prone to consider simultaneously all the facts, and to evaluate propositions with reference to specific individuals. The economist will argue that people are deterred by higher damage awards from acting negligently, all other things constant. The lawyer will counter with the claim that Mrs M., the defendant in the case, would not have taken more care because she did not think about the law or was not even aware of it at the time. The economist will counter that one does not have to show that *every* individual will be deterred, only that, on average, individuals will be, and, moreover, that particular

[1] R. H. Bork, 'New Constitutional Theories Threaten Rights, Bork Warns', *AEI Memorandum*, No. 44, Washington DC: AEI, 1985, p. 8.

[2] L. L. Fuller, *Anatomy of Law*, New York: Praeger, 1968, p. 4.

instances do not refute the theory because the evidence that could conceivably support the proposition would not come to the attention of lawyers—that is, a lower case-load and fewer people acting negligently.

At the root of the lawyer's criticism is a confusion of theory with description. Lawyers too often confuse their task with that of the judge. They analyse the law using the same language, reasoning and categories as judges and, therefore, are trapped into seeing the law in the same narrow way. When applied to developing a theoretical framework for the law it is doomed to failure since it inevitably gives the same answers and the same reasons as judges do. This approach will never reveal startling insights nor cut through the complexity and confusion of reality.

Economic Modelling

Economics, on the other hand, adopts a scientific approach. Economists think in terms of models and use simplifying assumptions to make complex problems manageable. These models are often criticised as being unrealistic. Of course they are! What possible benefit could there be in recreating reality in a more formal way? The answer must be none. A model's value is the way it sheds new insights on what were before confused and complicated matters, to reveal the connections between disparate areas and to unearth the 'common ground'.

Models are based on assumptions and assumptions by their nature are unrealistic. Lawyers frequently argue that the economics of law is based on unrealistic and over-simplified models. Here we must pause to consider the nature of theory, especially positive theory. Positive economic theory is a set of generalisations used to predict the consequences of change. There is one school of thought in economics, led by Milton Friedman, which claims that it is never legitimate to criticise a theory because its assumptions are unrealistic. The only way to evaluate a theory is to see whether its predictions, by which we mean its postulated relationships, are supported by empirical evidence. Moreover, where two theories are equally capable of explaining the same observations, the simpler is to be preferred. This is because theory and science seek generality. The more assumptions that are employed and the more specific the theory, the less general it will become and the less it will explain.

In short, *theory must be simple and unrealistic*. Its value lies in revealing connections hitherto unknown and in giving its possessor a compass to guide him through the (mostly irrelevant) complexity of the real world. As Professor Friedman has stated:

'A fundamental hypothesis of science is that appearances are deceptive and that there is a way of looking at or interpreting or organizing the evidence that will reveal superficially disconnected and diverse phenomena to be manifestations of a more fundamental and relatively simple structure.'[1]

Assumption of Rationality

Economics is based on the premise that people, on average, behave in a rational, self-interested way. It is, to quote Professor George Stigler, 'a stupendous palace erected on the granite of self-interest'.[2] This assumption means no more than that people act purposively in pursuit of their self-chosen ends: specifically, that people prefer more of the things they desire to less.

The assumption that people act rationally has been much maligned and ridiculed. It is argued that people are not rational, that they cannot and do not calculate, and that rationality imputes a degree of computational skill and knowledge that not even economists possess. Veblen's brutal parody of economic man is a classic statement of this class of criticism:

'. . . a lightning calculator of pleasures and pains, who oscillates like a homogeneous globule of . . . happiness under the impulse of stimuli that shift him about the area, but leave him intact'.[3]

Or Professor Kenneth Boulding's equally cutting dissection of 'economic man':

'It is a wonder indeed that economic institutions can survive at all, when economic man is so universally unpopular. No one in his senses would want his daughter to marry an economic man, one who counted every cost and asked for every reward, was never afflicted with mad generosity or uncalculating love, and who never acted out of a sense of inner identity, and indeed had no inner identity even if he was occasionally affected by carefully calculated considerations of benevolence or malevolence. The attack on economics is an attack on calculatedness, and the very fact that we think of calculating as

[1] M. Friedman, 'The Methodology of Positive Economics', in his *Essays in Positive Economics*, Chicago: University of Chicago Press, 1953, p. 33.

[2] G. J. Stigler, *The Economist as Preacher*, Oxford: Blackwell, 1989 (paperback edn.), p. 136.

[3] T. Veblen, 'Why Is Economics Not an Evolutionary Science?' (1898), in *The Place of Science in Modern Civilization*, New York, 1919, p. 73.

cold, suggests how exposed economists are to romantic and heroic criticism.'[1]

These criticisms are caricatures which disguise more sophisticated ways of looking at this assumption. I will suggest several.

If people do not behave in predictable ways, then the idea that we can regulate society by laws and incentives becomes untenable. Yet the whole basis of business, law and social activity is the assumption that people on average do respond in predictable ways. We know, for example, that when the price of a certain make of car increases relative to others, fewer of those cars are bought. The assumption of rationality is used by economists not as a description of all human behaviour but as a way of identifying the predictable component of the response of the average individual in a group. This use of the rationality assumption conceives of economic man as a weighted average of the group of individuals under investigation. It thus allows for marked differences in individual responses.

The second way of looking at the assumption of rationality is to ask what model of man we regard as the most appropriate one for framing laws. Can we safely assume that all men are good citizens and altruistic, or should we guard against the worst possible outcome by assuming that men are selfish and seek to maximise only their own welfare? Some legal and political theorists have argued that the latter assumption should be employed. Oliver Wendell Holmes argued that:

'If you want to know the law and nothing else, you must look at it as a bad man, who cares only for the material consequences which such knowledge enables him to predict, not as a good one, who finds his reasons for conduct, whether inside the law or outside of it, in the vaguer sanctions of the conscience.'[2]

What Holmes is saying here (in my view) is not that all men are bad, or that men only obey the law because they fear the consequences, but that this is a prudent model of man upon which to frame laws. Thus one can consistently hold the view that man is by nature law-abiding but that the best model of man to base our laws on is that we should constrain 'bad men'. This idea goes back even further to the 17th-century political philosopher, Thomas Hobbes, who said in *The Leviathan* (1661):

[1] K. E. Boulding, 'Economics as a Moral Science', *American Economic Review*, Vol. 68, 1968, p. 10.

[2] O. W. Holmes, 'The Path of the Law', *Harvard Law Review*, Vol. 10, 1897, p. 478.

'In constraining any system of government, and fixing the several checks and controls on the constitution, every man ought to be supposed a knave, and to have no other end, in all his actions, than private interest.'

Hedonistic Analysis of Law?

Economic analysis of law has been called 'dehumanising', a 'mechanical, hedonistic analysis of legal relationships'. In large part this is an inevitable consequence of an economic approach that emphasises trade-offs (the principle of substitution at the margin), which is instrumental (relates ends to their means of attainment) and which seeks to make explicit choices that are implicit and so generally go unrecognised. In practice, it is astounding how rarely lawyers and civil servants are prepared to state clearly the goal of a law or to assess the extent to which specific laws have achieved their intended results. The approach is usually in terms of definitions, procedures and wording, rather than costs, benefits and results. Ask any lawyer or civil servant what evidence exists or research has been undertaken on the effects of the criminal laws, policing, or health and safety legislation: How much has it cost? How many lives/crimes have been saved/prevented? Is it effective?—questions which receive only quizzical looks and a collective shrug of the shoulders.

It is precisely these questions which economics addresses and which alienate lawyers and lawmakers. But while lawyers and policy-makers can reject the economist's answers, they cannot ignore them. Every law, indeed every moral question, involves a choice, entails a trade-off *and* hence gives rise to a cost. Economists make the conditions of these legal and moral choices explicit.

Sometimes it is suggested that what really separates lawyers and economists is justice. Economists are interested in economic efficiency; lawyers, and the law, in justice. This distinction has some truth, but turns out on closer examination to be largely semantic.

The *Concise Oxford Dictionary* defines justice as 'fairness; exercise of authority in maintenance of a right'. Thus, when it is claimed that the law seeks justice, all that is being contended is that the authority of the law is being exercised to protect and enforce the rights defined by law. This is circular. The word 'justice' has no ethical content when used in this way. It tells us

[36]

nothing of the value or morality of specific legal rights. As Steven Lucas in *On Justice* states:

> 'the formal idea of equality or justice as a lodestar of social policy is devoid of all meaning, it is possible to advance every kind of postulate in the name of justice'.[1]

Professional Jargon

Economists do, however, have a serious problem of communication. Their treatment of law appears strained because it uses the metaphors and prose of the market-place. Many articles applying economics to law, model by analogy with the market. For example, the economist will talk about the 'supply of and demand for' crime, the penalty as a 'price' to engage in crime, thereby conveying the impression he believes that if criminals are willing to 'pay' an appropriate 'price' they can rape and pillage at will.

Two comments are apposite. First, economic metaphors are deeply embedded in the moral language used to describe crime and punishment: 'pay the price for his misdeeds', 'reap his rewards', 'the wages of sin', 'pay his debt to society', and so on. Also, the predominant sanction of the civil common law is financial damages, while the fine is the cornerstone of the Anglo-American penal system. These sanctions can be viewed as a penalty or, alternatively, as a price for engaging in an illegal activity, just as the price of a loaf of bread can be viewed as measuring its value, giving producers a reward and incentive to produce bread, penalising the consumer who buys bread for making a call on society's scarce resources and deterring those from consuming bread who do not value it very highly or cannot afford it. Just because something is called a price, a penalty, or a civil or criminal sanction, should not seduce us into thinking that the different labels necessarily carry analytical and behavioural differences.

Secondly, economists should not be taken literally. They, like other professions and 'experts', have fallen victim to jargon and acronym. The language of market analysis is frequently used to organise analysis, as a shorthand to distinguish the main factors relevant to the economic appraisal of a particular issue. But it is not the claim of economists that a 'market', say, in crime exists or should exist, only that there exists a 'supply' of criminal offences and a desire on the part of the prospective victims and society to prevent those crimes.

[1] S. Lucas, *On Justice*, Oxford: Clarendon Press, 1989, p. 31.

IV. LAW AS AN INCENTIVE SYSTEM

Economists see law as a system for altering incentives; lawyers see it as a set of rules and procedures. This is a fundamental distinction.

Ex Post versus Ex Ante

Lawyers typically take a retrospective view. Their factual inquiry begins with a dispute which must be resolved by the application of legal principles as distilled from the decisions in past cases. Since the lawyer comes to a problem after the dispute has arisen, it is natural that he should focus on the question of how it is to be resolved and how the solution affects the welfare of the parties directly involved.

The economist, on the other hand, is not so much concerned with the effect of the decision on the welfare of the parties to a dispute, as with the wider repercussions of the law on all potential litigants and individuals likely to find themselves in similar circumstances. His factual inquiry starts well before the dispute when both parties had the opportunity to re-organise their activities so as to minimise the possibility of a dispute, and the costs and harm that it would inflict. The law is seen as a method of re-allocating losses which provide incentives to people to reduce harm and use resources more efficiently.

Once it is recognised that the judge (as the 'creator' of laws) and the legislator can influence the allocation of resources, legal judgements and regulations can be examined for their incentive effects. In tort the issue confronting the courts usually involves a past loss—for example, a negligent driver fails to stop at a red light and damages another vehicle. This loss cannot, obviously, be avoided. It can only be *shifted* by the judge. But the judicial shifting of losses has effects on future victims and injurers, either by altering their behaviour or their post-injury decision whether to litigate or settle the case out of court. Thus, while the lawyer will focus on the actions of the parties to an accident to allocate 'fault', the economist will examine the impact of the way the court's decisions affect the accident rate, accident costs and the court's case-load. Moreover, the way the law alters behaviour is

[38]

often not directly observed by the lawyer, nor indeed is it part of the lawyer's experience. If the law is successful in deterring wrongdoing, accidents or crime, it means a legal dispute has been avoided. In short, successful laws mean less business for lawyers. It is therefore not surprising that they should give this part of the law less attention.

This simple difference of view explains a large part of the wide gap between economic and legal reasoning. Lawyers are concerned with the aftermath of the general conflict of interests and activities which inevitably occurs in society. The economist is concerned with the effect that rules have on behaviour *before* the mishap. The economist normally thinks of altering and tilting the incentives confronting individuals. In short, to quote Professor Lawrence Friedman:

> 'The basic idea of economic theory is that the legal system is a giant pricing machine ... When laws grant rights, or impose duties, they make behaviour of one sort or another cheaper or more expensive.'[1]

Rent Control and All That

Perhaps the best documented example of the incentive effects of law is rent control. The belief underlying rent control legislation is that by controlling the price of a commodity society can assist tenants by giving them cheaper accommodation. But economics informs us that controlling rents decreases the real rate of return to landlords, forcing them to seek other ways of increasing the income from their properties. They will, initially, try to get around controls by requiring 'key' or 'deposit' money, or by placing on tenants the obligation to repair and maintain the property. If these terms are also controlled, landlords will either withdraw their properties from rented accommodation or allow the quality of their properties to deteriorate by not maintaining them. The result of this type of legal intervention is that tenants as a group are harmed by shortages of rented accommodation or by the poor quality of the accommodation which is available.

The late Professor Arthur Leff captures the essence of the economist's approach to such subjects:

> 'There is an old widow, see, with six children. It is December and the weather is rotten. She defaults on the mortgage on her (and the babies') family home. The mortgagee, twirling his black moustache, takes the requisite legal steps to foreclose the mortgage and throw

[1] L. M. Friedman, 'Two Faces of Law', *Wisconsin Law Review*, No. 1, 1984, pp. 13-33.

them all out into the cold. She pleads her total poverty to the judge. Rising behind the bench, the judge points her and her brood out into the swirling blizzard. "Go", he says. "Your plight moves me not." "How awful", you say?

'"Nonsense", says the economi[st]. . . . ["L]ook at the other side of the . . . coin. What would happen if the judge let the old lady stay on just because she was out of money? First of all, lenders would in the future be loathe to lend to old widows with children. I don't say they wouldn't lend at all, they'd just be more careful about marginal cases, and raise the price of credit for the less marginal cases. The aggregate cost to the class of old ladies with homesteads would most likely rise more than the cost imposed on this particular widow. That is, the aggregate value of all their homes (known as their wealth) would fall, and they'd all be worse off".

'More than that, look at what such a decision would do to the motivation of old widows. Knowing that their failure to pay their debts would not be visited with swift retribution, they would have less incentive to prevent defaults. They might start giving an occasional piece of chicken to the kids, or even work up a fragment of beef from time to time. Profligacy like that would lead to even less credit-worthiness as their default rates climb. More and more of them would be priced out of the money market until no widow could ever *decide for herself* to mortgage her house to get the capital necessary to start a seamstress business to pull herself (and her infants) out of poverty. What do you mean, "awful"? What have you got against widows and orphans?"[1]

Costs and Benefits

Economics places at the forefront of discussion the costs and benefits of the law, considerations that will always be relevant when resources are limited. All too often, lawyers (politicians, pressure groups and civil servants) discuss the law as if it were costless. Economics informs us that nothing is free from the view-point of society as a whole. Increasing access to the courts, for example, consumes resources that will not then be available for other uses. While efficiency is not everything, the economic approach can nonetheless assist in determining whether, in allocating resources among competing uses, society is 'getting value for money'. As Leff succinctly puts it:

'the central tenet and most important operative principle of

[1] A. A. Leff, 'Economic Analysis of Law: Some Realism about Nominalism', *Virginia Law Review*, Vol. 60, 1976, p. 460.

economic analysis is to ask of every move (1) how much will it cost?;
(2) who pays?; and (3) who ought to decide both questions?'.[1]

Or more appositely by the Australian Law Commission:

'Law reform, and indeed law-making generally, must be alert to the
economic implications of their endeavour. The costs as well as the
benefits of legal change need to be weighed carefully and, where
possible, more scientifically than at present.'[2]

In this context economics has two applications. *Cost-benefit
analysis* seeks to measure both the costs and the benefits in
monetary terms. *Cost-effectiveness* attempts to achieve pre-stated
goals in the least costly fashion: getting more for less! The
economist adopting this approach is, to quote George Stigler,
merely 'a political arithmetician ... simply pointing out to the
society that what it seeks it is seeking inefficiently'.[3]

There is a great amount of confusion about what is meant by
cost-benefit analysis or economic efficiency. It is widely believed
that economists are obsessed with financial costs and benefits to
the exclusion of all else. This is not the case. Accountants deal
with financial costs and profits, not economists. Economists are
concerned with choice and resource allocation, and their
definition of cost is radically *subjective* and intimately related to
individual choices operating within the forces of demand and
supply.[4] This is why a theory which predicts people's reactions
to changes in the factors affecting benefits and costs is so central to
economics. Without the ability to anticipate the way consumers
and suppliers will react to changes, it would not be possible to
quantify the gains and losses of laws and regulations.

Willingness to Pay

In order to evaluate an activity which produces a variety of
benefits we must have some common measuring rod. Economists use money. But we must be clear not to confuse the way
economists measure benefits with the purely financial aspects of
a problem. The economic benefits are measured by the

[1] Leff, *op. cit.*

[2] Law Reform Commission, *Annual Report 1981*, Canberra: Australian Government
Publishing Service, 1981, p. 1.

[3] G. J. Stigler, *The Economist as Preacher, op. cit.*, p. 8.

[4] For one of the best discussions of costs, A. A. Alchian, *Economic Forces at Work*,
Indianapolis: Liberty Fund, 1977, Ch. 12.

'willingness-to-pay' of those individuals who are affected. That is, the economist's notion of benefit is similar to the utilitarian notion of happiness, but it is happiness backed by willingness-to-pay. Mere desire or 'need' is not relevant. The willingness-to-pay measure seeks to provide a quantitative indication of an individual's *intensity* of preferences.

Consider two examples where the measures of financial and economic benefit differ.

o In many markets identical goods frequently sell for the same price to all customers. It follows that individuals with an intense preference for the good (i.e., who would be prepared to pay more) are receiving a substantial benefit from their purchase which is not measured in the market. Moreover, this surplus benefit is not captured as additional profit to the manufacturer. The economist calls this benefit *consumer's surplus*—the difference between the maximum sum an individual would be willing to pay and the sum he actually pays. It is the analogue for the consumer of economic profit to the firm. The goal of an efficient economic system is to maximise the joint surplus of consumers and manufacturers, not the market price and not money profits. In fact, the economic goal of a market is to maximise consumer welfare.

o Economists appreciate that decisions are made on the basis of both monetary and non-monetary attributes. Take, for example, the choice of a job. An individual does not accept a job solely on the basis of its wage or salary, but the whole package of benefits which go with it—the fringe benefits, working conditions, prospects of advancement, security of employment, travel, the reputation of the firm or institution, its location, and so on. As a result, people are willing to trade money for more of these attractive factors. Thus academic lawyers are paid substantially less than practising solicitors, and presumably they remain academics because the total non-monetary benefits exceed the higher salary they could earn in practice. Looked at another way, they are paying for the privilege of consuming these benefits in terms of the forgone salary.

The economist deals with this situation by measuring the non-monetary benefits in terms of the money that the individual gives up. That is, there is a 'monetary equivalent' of these benefits which, when added to the pecuniary salary, gives us the money value of the total package of benefits received from employment in a particular job. That is done not because the money itself is valuable—in fact, it has no intrinsic economic value for an economist—but rather because it provides a simple means of comparing diverse attributes and alternatives.

Valuing Intangibles[1]

It is frequently argued that many aspects of life cannot be reduced to a monetary value—the so-called intangibles of freedom, life, love and the environment. It would be fruitless to deny that these are non-economic in character and often not traded in the market. But it would be equally foolish to suppose that the point undermines economic analysis. Many intangibles can be valued in monetary terms, and are implicitly done so by individuals and society daily. Take the example of personal safety. Much of the civil law deals with personal injury litigation involving loss of life and limb. It is often said that life is priceless, that it does not have a monetary value and that any attempt to give it one is evil. Two observations should be made.

First, if life is regarded as priceless by individuals and society, we would never observe people taking any action involving personal risk. Something which has an infinite value must be preserved at any cost! But we, and the people around us, take risks every day, some quite substantial. The plain fact is that the actions of individuals imply that they do not regard their life as priceless, and are willing to trade the *risk* of death for material and psychic benefits. Secondly, our social institutions do 'price' life. In tort we do not kill the person who negligently takes the life of another, we require only that he/she pays compensation. Look at it in a slightly different way: the law is in effect saying that you can kill a person through negligence so long as you are willing to pay the 'price'. If society really did regard life as 'priceless', would it adopt such a lax response—as it does in courtrooms every day—to situations where it is believed that the individual could have prevented a fatal accident if only more care had been taken?

---

[1] For methods of valuing intangibles, D. W. Pearce and A. Markandya, *Environmental Policy Benefits: Monetary Valuation*, Paris: OECD, 1989; D. Pearce, A. Markandya and E. B. Barber, *Blueprint for a Green Economy*, London: Earthscan Publications, 1989.

The Economics of Safety

This last example provides a good illustration of the way economists link monetary valuation to resource allocation. Economists value life and limb in order to determine how much to invest in safety.

The economist does not ask the question: How much would you pay to stay alive? He asks the more subtle question: How much are you willing to pay to reduce the risk of death given that you do not know when and if you will be killed? That is the amount of money the individual is willing to pay to reduce the *risk* of death.

The economist's willingness-to-pay procedure can be explained in the following way. You cross a busy road each morning which is dangerous. You can cross it in one of two ways—by using a pedestrian crossing which adds five minutes to your travel time or by waiting for a gap in the traffic and rushing across. The latter action increases the likelihood of you being killed by one in a million—a small risk by all accounts. If you valued your own life at an infinite amount you would not take the risk, nor, indeed, *any* risks. This is because you would be comparing an infinite loss against a finite cost of taking greater care. But we observe people taking these risks every day and some dying as a result. What are we to make of such actions? It is this. People, in deciding what care they will take, compare the costs of greater precautions against the risks, and are willing to trade improvements in their material welfare for decreases or increases in risks. A pedestrian's decision not to use a crossing implicitly trades time for risk. *Ex ante*, this trade seems reasonable and from it we can derive the value that the group taking such action places on a statistical death.

Let me illustrate how one would make such a calculation. Suppose the saving in time to each person from not using the pedestrian crossing is 60 pence and the increase in risk is one in a million, the decision not to use the crossing implies a value of at least £600,000. Put differently, the value of a pedestrian crossing which saves one statistical life is £600,000. It is, therefore, economically worthwhile to spend up to £600,000 to construct such a crossing.

There is a more general principle to be derived from the economics of safety. It is an answer to, or at least some guidance on, the vexing question of 'How safe is safe?' and, in the case of tort law, discussed later, 'What is reasonable care?'. Even though many risks could be totally avoided, the costs to society would be prohibitive in terms of direct safety costs and losses in output, jobs and even pleasure if we include sports which are often fraught with great personal risks (mountain climbing, boxing). Cost considerations limit society's willingness to avoid all risks.

There exists an optimal amount of safety which is defined by the costs and benefits of risk reduction. Many risks (accidents) can be reduced by taking more care, but only at a higher cost. The economic problem is to locate the point where the costs of more safety are balanced by the reduction in expected accident losses. Optimal care is achieved when an additional pound spent on reducing risks saves one pound in *expected* accident losses. Optimal defined in this way means that many accidents are 'justified'—because they would be too costly to avoid. The corollary to this is that, just as there can be too little care, there can also be excessive care.

The idea of a market for safety is by no means novel or farfetched. Adam Smith argued that more hazardous jobs, other things equal, pay higher wages than safer jobs. The wage premium of the hazardous job implicitly compensates the worker for running the risk of injury or death and, simultaneously, gives an incentive to the employer to provide greater safety. The employer's return from providing greater safety is in the form of a lower wage bill. This idea of an implicit market for safety has been increasingly subjected to empirical investigation, and the evidence provides support for the idea.[1]

By framing the question in terms of resource allocation, the economist is able to adopt a consistent valuation procedure—one which can be used to assist policy-makers by offering a consistent criterion for allocating resources to saving lives.

Opportunity Costs

The discussion of economic benefits has transgressed on the economist's concept of opportunity costs. What is a benefit to one person is often a cost to another.

The economic cost of a thing is its value in the next best, forgone alternative use. If I produce a good, the costs of production not only reflect my outlay on labour, plant and materials but the profit I sacrifice in not using those resources in

---

[1] C. G. Veljanovski, 'Regulating Industrial Accidents: An Economic Analysis of Market and Legal Responses', York, D.Phil., 1982; C. G. Veljanovski, 'The Valuation of Injury in Economics and Law', London: Department of Transport, 1989 (mimeo).

their next best use. It follows that the notion of economic profit makes an allowance for a 'normal' rate of return on capital (for example, what you could earn by keeping the money in a safe bank account).[1] It therefore should not be confused with profits as measured by the accountants. Clearly, if the next best use of my resources is more profitable than their current use, then I am earning economic losses, not profits—even though I am showing an accounting profit. The prudent investor would realise this, and re-allocate his activities to their highest-valued uses. This is why economists assert, apparently paradoxically, that under perfect competition firms earn no 'economic' profits.

It is important not to confuse accounting or historical costs with economic costs. If you bought a house for £5,000 six years ago and are now offered £20,000, the cost of the house is £20,000, not £5,000. It is £20,000 because that is what you are now giving up to remain in the house, so that the £20,000 reflects the house's next best alternative use. Economists cost things in this way because they are concerned with the way resources are allocated, and want to ensure that resources are allocated to their highest-valued uses.

The Coase Theorem Revisited

The concept of opportunity costs is the bedrock of the Coase Theorem (discussed above, p. 22) and much of the new economics of law. Take as an example the 1879 case of *Sturgess v. Bridgeman* discussed by Coase.[2] A confectioner in Wigmore Street used two mortars and pestles, one being in operation in the same position for over 60 years. This caused his neighbour—a doctor—no bother for eight years until he built a consulting room at the end of his garden right next to the confectioner's kitchen. The noise and vibration made it difficult for the doctor to use the consulting room. The doctor sued the confectioner claiming that the noise was excessive.

Will what the court decides affect the use of these two plots of land? Coase's answer is 'no', provided the doctor and confectioner can negotiate.

To establish this we need to assign monetary values to the gains and losses of both parties. Assume that the profit from making confectionery is £400 and that the loss of profit inflicted

[1] J. Edwards *et al.*, *The Economic Analysis of Accounting Profitability*, Oxford: Oxford University Press, 1987.

[2] (1879), 4, C.P.D. 172.

on the doctor is £300. The efficient solution is for the confectioner to continue using his machinery (a gain of £400 minus £300 = £100).

Suppose that the court decides, in flagrant disregard of the economics, to award the doctor an injunction which requires the confectioner to cease the noise. You may argue that this will freeze the land in an inefficient use. But you would be wrong. If the court, as it did, awards the injunction, the confectioner has an incentive to bargain with the doctor to, in effect, 'buy out' of the injunction. In terms of the figures which have been assigned, the doctor only values peace and quiet at £300, whereas the confectioner values productive noise at £400. A mutually advantageous bargain can be struck between them—the confectioner would be willing to pay the doctor up to £400 for something the doctor values at only £300. There is thus a bargaining range of £100 where some agreement can be reached, although the exact payment cannot be predicted since it depends on the bargaining abilities of the parties. The injunction forms only the starting point for negotiation; it does not influence the pattern of land use.

If the case had been decided the other way, the judicially imposed solution would be the final solution and it would, on the figures assumed, be the efficient solution. Since the doctor has not got his injunction he must, if he wants less noise, bargain with the confectioner. But, since his loss is only £300 and the confectioner's profit is £400, he cannot offer the confectioner a sum sufficient to induce him to stop using his mortars and pestles.

From this example we can see that two totally antithetical rules of law lead to the same solution, and that in both cases the person inflicting the harm has taken into account the losses of the victim. The confectioner 'bears' the loss irrespective of the legal position. When he is liable, and even if the remedy is an injunction as opposed to damages, he bears the cost of harm in the sum he pays the doctor. If the harm is not an actionable nuisance, then the cost of the damage he inflicts on the doctor is taken into account by the payment he refuses. This is because he could readily convert his legal right into cash. The fact that he does not is a forgone sum, an opportunity cost. As Coase himself put it, in economics 'the receipt forgone of a given amount is the equivalent of a payment of the same amount'.[1]

[1] Coase, 'The Problem of Social Costs', *op. cit.*, p. 7.

Implications of Opportunity Cost Analysis

This discussion of costs and bargaining may seem irrelevant to lawyers, if only because in many situations the parties cannot bargain. But several important economic truths are illustrated by Coase's discussion.

First, the economist's cost/benefit analysis is not confined to financial costs and accounting profits, but has a much wider ambit. It has to do with choice, with the balancing of competing claims on scarce resources. The economist's efficiency goal seeks to maximise the joint gain or to minimise the joint loss to individuals. A lawyer would call this balancing the interests of the plaintiff and the defendant. But these different ways of expressing the problem recognise that, if we make a decision in favour of one party, we harm the other. The question is: On what basis do we make the decision having regard to the parties' interests and rights? The economist offers a technical algorithm: evaluate all the advantages and disadvantages in money terms to both parties and minimise the sum of the joint costs—or, what is the same, maximise the sum of net benefits.

Secondly, Coase subtly undermined the notion that the physical causation of harm is pertinent to the economics of market failure, and that this is recognised by the common law. The claim 'A hurt B' has no economic relevance. The harm results from the proximity of two incompatible activities— remove one and the harm disappears. Losses are therefore the result of the interaction of two conflicting or interfering activities and are properly to be treated as the *joint cost* of both activities. This is also true of the expenses incurred to settle claims arising from such disputes. This line of reasoning suggests that all victims are partly the 'authors' of their own misfortune. In the allocative sense this is correct. In terms of the legal choice that has to be made, the 'harm' is reciprocal in character: to permit the defendant to continue is to harm the plaintiff; to decide in favour of the plaintiff inflicts harm on the defendant. The economist uses the word 'costs' where the lawyer would use 'interest'. But that should not mislead us. The economist's balancing of costs and benefits is no different from the judgemental process engaged in by the courts in resolving most legal disputes.

Thirdly, Coase's analysis emphasises the importance of transaction costs as a principal determinant of the law's effect on economic activity and behaviour. Transaction costs can be

[48]

defined as the costs of information and bargaining, and of defining, policing and enforcing property rights and contracts. In short, they are the frictions associated with transacting. Coase suggested that many institutions—among them, the firm, commodity exchanges and contracts—can be explained as efficient adaptations to transaction costs. Transaction costs block mutually beneficial exchange and co-operation. In *Sturgess v. Bridgeman* they would have fixed land in inefficient uses if the judge had decided incorrectly. If transaction costs are sufficiently high the law will have economic effects and the investigator must turn to an identification of the source and size of transaction costs properly to analyse the law and possible reform. It is no exaggeration to say that the intellectual bridge between law and economics has, as one of its main supporting arches, the notion of transaction costs.[1]

Fourthly, the economic function of law is not to prevent all harm but rather to balance the interests of the victim against the interests and welfare of the injurer and of consumers in general. In economic terms this means balancing the losses due to the harm and the costs of preventing the harm. When the sum of these costs is minimised we have the 'efficient' or 'optimal' level of harm. As the judge in *Daborn v. Bath Tramways* observed:

> 'As has been pointed out, if all the trains in this country were restricted to a speed of 5 miles an hour, there would be fewer accidents, but our national life would be intolerably slowed down.'

Only rarely will economic considerations lead to such extreme solutions as the complete elimination of pollution or accidents, even if such radical solutions were technically feasible.

Finally, the discussion points to the need to go beyond the law. In many legal settings the parties can bargain. When this is possible we must recognise that, after a law has been enacted, the parties will adjust their relationships and their contracts to offset the re-allocation of costs brought about by the law. Thus laws that make employers liable for injuries to their workers might not increase the costs to employers because wages might fall to offset damage payments. Likewise, making manufacturers liable for defective products might simply increase the price of goods without any improvement in safety or in consumer welfare. The lesson for lawyers is that individuals react to laws in ways which minimise the burdens those laws place upon them.

[1] O. Williamson, *The Economic Institutions of Capitalism*, New York: Free Press, 1985.

Quantitative Analysis

Lawyers are not very good with figures. As Professor Bob Cooter, of the University of California (Berkeley), has remarked:

'Left to its own devices, the law stood no more chance of developing quantitative methodology than Australia stood of developing the rabbit.'[1]

Economists have recently occupied this niche with great vigour. Specialist journals, such as *The Journal of Law and Economics* and *The Journal of Legal Studies*, are full of articles about the impact of no-fault laws on accident rates, the effects of regulation on economic variables, and more specific quantitative studies which have been used in litigation. Economists have at their disposal many sophisticated statistical techniques which can be used to quantify the impact of the law. Although not all legal questions are amenable to statistical analysis, those which are can be examined with more rigour and statistical validity (in the context of an explicitly formulated theory) through the use of economics.

There are a number of areas where economics can contribute to the work of lawyers and policy-makers.

Statistical analysis can be used to measure the impact of laws and to decide factual questions, for example, whether there has been discrimination in wages paid to females or those of different races, which are not accounted for by differences in productivity and other work characteristics; or whether prices charged for commodities are monopolistic or reflect differences in quality. Techniques, such as multiple-regression analysis— which are designed to disentangle the effects of different individual variables on aggregate data—are available, and can assist in factual inquiries.[2]

A great many laws are based on assumptions about their ability to deter anti-social behaviour and achieve desired goals. Surprisingly, there is little evidence, and no systematic research programme in the UK, to determine whether financial regulations benefit investors, whether safety laws actually protect

---

[1] R. D. Cooter, 'Law and the Imperialism of Economics: An Introduction to the Economic Analysis of Law and a Review of the Major Books', *UCLA Law Review*, Vol. 29, 1982, p. 1,260.

[2] F. M. Fisher, 'Multiple Regression in Legal Proceedings', *Columbia Law Review*, Vol. 80, 1980, pp. 702-36; D. L. Rubinfeld, 'Econometrics in the Courtroom', *Columbia Law Review*, Vol. 85, 1985, pp. 1,040-92.

workers and consumers, or whether criminal sanctions deter crime (see pp. 55-63). This tally of our ignorance on fundamental questions such as these can be expanded almost without limit. When attempts have been made to examine the impact of laws, the findings have been disappointing. The intended effects, such as the presumed ability of industrial safety legislation to improve job safety, are usually so small as to be undetectable. On the other hand, the direct costs and such indirect ones as, for example, investment and productivity, and inefficiency, are generally significant. (This is discussed at greater length in Section VI.)

In other countries, such as North America and Australia, more systematic evaluations of the impact of law reform are undertaken to guide policy-makers.[1] In the UK, despite the greater weight given to economics in recent years, little attempt is made to justify laws in cost-benefit terms. Elsewhere, I and others have drawn attention to major examples of reform in financial and company law which have rejected any requirement to ground proposals in well-reasoned economic terms.[2] Legal impact studies can make an important contribution to legal and regulatory policy by providing the policy-maker with much-needed information on the effects of law.

[1] B. Braddock, *Product Liability: Economic Impacts*, Australian Law Reform Commission, Product Liability Research Paper, No. 2, 1989.

[2] C. G. Veljanovski, 'Introduction' in A. Seldon (ed.), *Financial Regulation – Or Over-Regulation?*, IEA Readings 27, London: IEA, 1988.

V. SOME LEGAL APPLICATIONS

So far the discussion has been very general. It is now time to put some flesh on the economics of law by discussing some specific applications.

The Roles of the Economist

(a) Technician

The economist has at least three roles in legal analysis.[1] The first is that of *technician*. This is to accept the legal problem as formulated by lawyers and to seek to solve it by applying economics. Company A breaches its contract with B for the supply of machinery resulting in lost profits to B: What is the correct basis on which to calculate the lost profits? In UK and European competition laws the definition of the 'relevant market' often requires the skills of an economist to identify barriers to entry, the degree of cross-elasticity between similar products which would class them as economic substitutes, and the extent of competition between sellers.[2] These issues give the economist scope to assist lawyers and regulators without in any way challenging their approach or authority.

(b) Supertechnician

The second role is that of the *supertechnician*. Here the economist treats an area of law as if its objective were to improve the allocation of resources in the economy. Rent control is a good example. Economics is used to identify the effects of rent control on the costs, supply and quality of rented accommodation, and on productivity and growth, and having determined these effects, to compare the costs of the legislation with its benefits. This often requires cutting through the legal language and basis of the law, in order to focus on its economic impact.

---

[1] These categories are taken from A. Klevorick, 'Law and Economic Theory: An Economist's View', reprinted in Ogus and Veljanovski, *op. cit.*, pp. 31-37.

[2] The recent White Paper on restrictive practices states: 'What is the "relevant market" for a particular product or service will be established through economic analysis.' Department of Trade & Industry, *Opening Markets: New Policy on Restrictive Trade Practices*, Cm. 727, 1989, para. 2.12.

(c) Economic Rhetorician

The economist's third role is what may be termed that of *economic rhetorician*. This role employs economic concepts and terms to provide a new vocabulary for lawyers. It can take the form of a full-blown efficiency analysis such as Judge Posner's hypothesis that the common law can be explained as if judges were trying to bring about a more efficient allocation of resources. Alternatively, economic principles can be used to organise the discussion of the decisions of judges—categorising them, drawing out the common threads, defining legal terms more clearly, and criticising the logic of legal decisions and laws by pointing to inconsistencies in reasoning, and so on. In other words, the economist is here using economics to make general propositions about the law in a way lawyers would find intuitively acceptable.

Personal Injury Damages

Consider first the economist as a technician. Under English common law the object of the award of damages to a negligently injured plaintiff is to provide 'full compensation' in the sense of placing the person in the same position that he or she would have been in had the injury not occurred, in so far as money can. The economist, actuary and accountant can all assist the court in achieving the goal of full compensation defined in this way. Yet, surprisingly, the English judiciary has discouraged expert evidence in personal injury and death cases, preferring a relatively unsophisticated arithmetical calculation which has the effect of severely under-compensating the victims of accidents.

This is particularly so for future losses. Many accident victims suffer continuing losses which impair their ability to work full-time or as productively as before the accident. In such cases the judge must estimate the future lost stream of income and then discount it by some interest rate to arrive at a fixed sum to award the victim as 'full' compensation. Instead of using economic and actuarial evidence, the courts use a *multiplier/multiplicand* approach. This has two parts. First, the judge must determine the victim's annual loss arising from the accident. This is a question of fact.[1] The court must then convert this annual sum into the present value of the plaintiff's prospective loss. The judge does this by first determining a multiplier which he uses to multiply the victim's annual loss. The multiplier takes into account two

[1] Kemp & Kemp, *The Quantum of Damages*, London: Sweet & Maxwell, 1988.

[53]

factors—discounting and an allowance for what are frequently referred to as the 'vicissitudes of life'. Discounting is required to adjust for the fact that the victim is in early receipt of his compensation and can invest it over the remaining period of his life to earn an annuity. The courts also adjust future loss downwards to take account of contingencies which would reduce the loss attributable to the accident, such as remarriage, the prospect of unemployment, and the likelihood of illnesses which could shorten life. These factors are not explicitly taken into account in any principled arithmetic fashion. Rather, the judge (juries have been abolished in England and Wales for civil trials except in libel actions) arrives at a figure which in his judgement provides adequate compensation. The multiplier used by the courts falls in the range of 5 to 18, although 15 is the maximum typically used.

The multipliers used by the courts are low, leading to severe under-compensation of accident victims. Indeed, most legal practitioners and judges remained ignorant of the discount rate implied by multipliers until Lord Diplock revealed that it was around 4 to 5 per cent.[1] Kemp and others have argued both for the increased use of actuarial evidence and for a discount rate of around 1·5 to 2·3 per cent per annum.[2]

An illustration of the degree of under-compensation is provided by the facts in the case of *Mitchell v. Mulholland*,[3] where Lord Justice Edmund Davies ruled that expert evidence of economists was inadmissible. Using the 'multiplier' approach, the Court of Appeal multiplied the plaintiff's net pre-trial loss of annual earnings by 14 to arrive at total damages of £20,833.

If an economist had been asked to compensate the plaintiff in *Mitchell v. Mulholland*, he would have ended up much better-off.[4] Using the plaintiff's annual net earnings at the time of injury (£1,255), and assuming that he worked until retirement at 65, that productivity grew at 1 per cent per year, and using a discount rate of 2 per cent, the estimated loss to the injured victim at the date of injury would have been £36,438. If interest

[1] *Cookson v. Knowles* (1979), A.C. 556 (H.L.).

[2] D. Kemp, 'The Assessment of Damages for Future Pecuniary Loss in Personal Injury Claims', *Civil Justice Quarterly*, 1984, pp. 120-32.

[3] [1971] 2 All E.R. 1205, C.A.

[4] A. M. Parkman, 'The Multiplier in English Fatal Accident Cases: What Happens When Judges Teach Economics?', *International Review of Law and Economics*, Vol. 5, 1985, pp. 187-97.

is added the figure increases to £48,262 at the time of trial in 1969, and to £54,243 at the time of the Court of Appeal decision in 1971. The final sum calculated using these reasonable assumptions is more than two-and-a-half times the sum awarded to the plaintiff by the court.

Here is an instance where simple economics can not only improve the consistency of the law but the welfare of accident victims. The fact that judges blatantly refuse to employ standard financial techniques, such as compound interest and sensible discounting rates, and persist in an approach that has obvious defects is one of those 'mysteries of the law'.

The Economics of Criminal Laws

Analysis of crime and the criminal law casts the economist in the roles of technician *and* supertechnician. As a technician the economist has produced a mass of empirical evidence to support the thesis that criminal penalties deter crime. As a super-technician the economist has suggested ways in which the criminal law and its procedures can be improved to increase their cost-effectiveness in crime prevention and the admin-istration of the system of criminal justice.

There can be little dispute that crime is an economic problem. In 1988 there were 3·6 million recorded offences in England and Wales. The total expenditure of the Home Office was £1,241 million, on police £8,277 million, on prisons £1,014 million, and on the courts £1,886 million. The costs of crime prevention to the private sector are unknown, as are the losses which the victims and the community suffer. Put simply, the material welfare of society would be considerably larger if crime did not exist.

The economic approach to crime is based on the assumption that criminals, victims and law enforcers are rational, that is, they all respond in predictable ways to changes in costs and benefits.[1] The decision to engage in crime is seen as no different in character from that of choosing a job. An individual participates in criminal activity because it offers a stream of net benefits greater than that of legitimate uses of his time and effort. 'Persons become "criminals",' states Becker, 'not because their

[1] This section is based on C. G. Veljanovski, 'The Economics of Criminal Law and Procedure', *Coexistence*, Vol. 23, 1986, pp. 137-53.

basic motivations differ from that of other persons, but because their benefits and costs differ.'[1]

Deterrence

If criminals are deterred by the penalties meted out by the law, then society must decide which type and at what level the penalties should be set. For the economist these matters will be determined by the extent to which different types of penalties (fines, imprisonment, community service, and so on) deter crime, compared to the respective costs of these sanctions.

The penalty which influences a criminal's actions and decision to participate in a crime is the product of two elements, the severity of the sanction and the frequency with which it is imposed on offenders. By multiplying these factors we obtain the *expected* penalty. Thus, if the penalty is a fine of £200 but only 50 per cent of offenders are apprehended and convicted, then the expected penalty is £100 ($0.5 \times £200 = £100$). If criminals are risk-neutral, that is, they evaluate risky prospects solely in terms of the expected value of an increase or decrease in their wealth, the same level of deterrence can be achieved by reducing either the level of the fine or its likelihood, provided there is a compensating increase in the other. Thus a 50 per cent chance of a £200 fine ($0.5 \times £200 = £100$) brings about the same level of deterrence as a 25 per cent prospect of a £400 fine ($0.25 \times £400 = £100$). In each case the expected fine is £100.

The optimal combination of the conviction rate and the severity of the penalty are, in the economic model, solely determined by the costs to society of using them. Apprehending and convicting offenders is very costly—it requires manpower, considerable time and equipment. Fines, on the other hand, deter by the *threat* that they will be imposed. Thus the costs of enforcing the criminal law and deterring crime can be lowered by progressively increasing the severity of the fine whilst reducing the conviction rate.

Cost of Punishment

Cost considerations also suggest the form punishment should take. It is always cheaper to use monetary fines than imprisonment or other custodial sanctions. Fines are easy to calculate and involve a simple transfer payment from the offender to the state

[1] G. S. Becker, 'Crime and Punishment: An Economic Approach', *Journal of Political Economy*, Vol. LXXVI, 1968, pp. 167-217.

which can be used to compensate the victim and defray the costs of the police and the courts. Imprisonment adds avoidable costs, such as the investment in prisons, the wages of warders and probationary officers, and the value of the offender's lost production in legitimate activities. Society gains nothing from this form of punishment when the alternative of costless monetary fines is available.

What has so far been outlined is the so-called 'case for fines'. This can be reduced to two propositions:

o The same level of deterrence can be achieved with a reduction in enforcement activity (policing, apprehension and prosecution) provided there is a compensating increase in the severity of punishment.

o Punishment should take the form, where possible, of high monetary fines because they deter crime costlessly. This general rule is qualified when prospective criminals are insolvent, when errors in conviction are frequently made, and where preferences toward risk differ high fines may deter socially desirable activity. The last is particularly true of regulatory and 'white-collar' crimes where lawbreaking is often associated with some otherwise productive activity. In these situations fines may be ineffective because they either do not deter (insolvent criminal), or run the risk of taxing innocence, or deterring the wrong activity. Moreover, uniformly high fines may lead to perverse incentives. If fines (or any sanctions) are draconian, prospective criminals will not be deterred from committing more heinous crimes. If stealing a loaf of bread or armed robbery both attract similar penalties, the law does little to discourage the more serious crime. Differential fines must, therefore, be built into the criminal penalty system. Also, severe penalties tend to be nullified by judges and juries. One argument against the death penalty is that juries are more likely to find the guilty innocent than run the risk of inflicting a death sentence on an innocent person.

Measuring Deterrence

Economists have not stopped at these general tenets. Beginning with the work of Professor Isaac Ehrlich[1] in the USA, there have

---

[1] I. Ehrlich, 'Participation in Illegitimate Activities: A Theoretical and Empirical Investigation', *Journal of Political Economy*, Vol. 81, 1973, pp. 521-64.

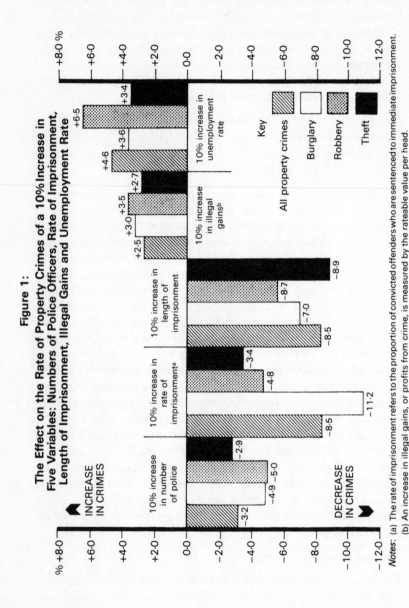

Figure 1:

The Effect on the Rate of Property Crimes of a 10% Increase in Five Variables: Numbers of Police Officers, Rate of Imprisonment, Length of Imprisonment, Illegal Gains and Unemployment Rate

Key

All property crimes

Burglary

Robbery

Theft

10% increase in number of police

10% increase in rate of imprisonment[a]

10% increase in length of imprisonment

10% increase in illegal gains[b]

10% increase in unemployment rate

INCREASE IN CRIMES

DECREASE IN CRIMES

Notes: (a) The rate of imprisonment refers to the proportion of convicted offenders who are sentenced to immediate imprisonment.
(b) An increase in illegal gains, or profits from crime, is measured by the rateable value per head.

Source: D. J. Pyle, 'The Economics of Crime in Britain', *Economic Affairs*, Vol. 9, No. 2, December 1988/January 1989, pp. 6–9.

been literally hundreds of statistical studies which broadly confirm the economist's deterrence model. Moreover, these studies have often provided estimates of the impact on crime of changes in enforcement activity and penalties.[1]

David Pyle, for example, has undertaken such a statistical study of property crime in England and Wales.[2] Within an explicitly formulated economic model of crime he has examined the impact on the incidence of property crime of changes in key enforcement variables (the number of police, conviction rate, and length of imprisonment), the economic gains from illegal activity, and the unemployment rate. The results support the predictions of the economic model; those variables which increased the expected penalty tended to reduce the incidence of property crimes while those which increased the gains to illegal activity or decreased the gains to legitimate activity have the opposite effect. Pyle's statistical findings are reproduced in Figure 1. They indicate the impact of a 10 per cent increase in each enforcement variable on the rate of property crime.

Results like those calculated by Pyle are a valuable input into evaluating the cost-effectiveness of different policies to reduce crime. In Table 1 the results of Pyle's statistical study are matched to the costs of each enforcement activity in achieving a 1 per cent reduction in the incidence of property crime. They show clearly that reducing crime by employing more police is *not* cost-effective. To achieve a 1 per cent reduction in property crime by greater policing would require an annual expenditure of over £51 million. This is 10 times the cost of achieving the same reduction through an increase in the imprisonment rate or the length of imprisonment.

Plea Bargaining

Economics can also be used to analyse legal procedure. Consider-able research has been undertaken to identify the factors which in-fluence the decision of individuals and companies to go to court or negotiate a settlement out of court. Since most cases are settled against the backdrop of trial, it is important to understand not only why this is so but how changes in legal costs and procedural rules will affect the court's case-load and the welfare of potential litigants.

[1] D. J. Pyle, *The Economics of Criminal Law and Law Enforcement*, London: Macmillan, 1983.

[2] D. J. Pyle, *An Economic Model of Recorded Property Crimes in England and Wales*, Ph.D. Thesis, University of Leicester, 1984; Pyle, 'The Economics of Crime in Britain', *Economic Affairs*, Vol. 9, No. 2, December 1988/January 1989, pp. 6-9.

TABLE 1

ESTIMATED COSTS OF REDUCING PROPERTY CRIMES BY ONE PER CENT

Policy option	Cost (£million)
Either Increase number of police officers[a]	51·2
or Increase number of people sentenced to imprisonment[b]	4·9
or Increase average length of imprisonment[b]	3·6

Notes: (a) The cost of employing an additional police officer is estimated as £16,000 per annum.

       (b) The cost of keeping someone in prison is estimated to be £15,000 per annum.

Source: D. J. Pyle, 'The Economics of Crime in Britain', *Economic Affairs*, Vol. 9, No. 2, December 1988/January 1989, pp. 6-9.

In the United States, and to a lesser extent in England and Wales, most civil cases are settled by pre-trial negotiations. This is also used in criminal law by means of what is called the 'plea bargain'. This is the practice whereby the defendant enters a plea of guilty in return for a lower sentence. In the United States plea bargaining is practised openly. It has been estimated that in 90 per cent of criminal cases a guilty plea is entered, and 50 per cent of these involve a bargain between the accused and the prosecutor. In England and Wales the legal profession and judges deny that the practice exists, although research shows that it is fairly prevalent.[1]

Plea bargaining has a straightforward economic explanation: the disposition of cases through pre-trial negotiation is cheaper and offers 'gains' to both prosecutor and defendant. The prosecutor faces an economic problem—how to allocate his limited resources to dispose of the maximum number of cases weighted by the sentences.[2] A rational prosecutor with discretion to decide how to deal with his case-load will set about his job in

[1] J. Baldwin and M. McConville, *Negotiated Justice—Pressure to Plead Guilty*, London: Martin Robertson, 1977.

[2] W. M. Landes, 'An Economic Analysis of the Courts', *Journal of Law & Economics*, Vol. XIV, 1970, pp. 61-108; R. P. Adelstein, 'The Plea Bargain in England and America: A Comparative Institutional View', in P. Burrows and C. G. Veljanovski (eds.), *The Economic Approach to Law*, London: Butterworth, 1981, Ch. 10.

the most cost-effective manner. Plea bargaining is one device which achieves this end. The prosecutor trades a lower sentence for the certainty of conviction, thereby saving the costs of 'proving' guilt beyond reasonable doubt. The accused is encouraged to plead guilty by trading the uncertainty of a trial which may impose a more severe sentence if he insists on pleading his innocence, with the certainty of a lower sentence if he pleads guilty. If the prosecutor's maximum sentence reduction equals or exceeds the defendant's minimum sentence discount, then a guilty plea will be entered. Cost factors drive both parties to seek a compromise through pre-trial settlement. The plea bargain, like the more common out-of-court settlement in civil trials, has an economic rationale. It forces individuals to reach voluntary agreements to settle their disputes—a cheaper procedure. This, in turn, enables the criminal justice system to function more smoothly. As the eminent legal academic, Professor Glanville Williams, states:

'... offenders who have no defence must be persuaded not to waste the time of the court and public money; pleas of guilty save the distress of witnesses in having to give evidence, as well as inconvenience and loss of time, and in the present conditions such pleas are essential to prevent serious congestion of the courts'.[1]

These explanations for the 'plea bargain' are by no means the unique insight of the economist. His contribution lies in generating additional predictions about how changes in the circumstances surrounding criminal trials will influence the outcome of plea bargains. According to the economist's models, the likelihood of going to trial will increase:

o the greater the disagreement over the trial outcome between defendant and prosecutor;

o the greater the severity of the crime as measured by the potential sentence;

o the more liberal the availability of legal aid to the defendant; and

o is inversely related to the length and unpleasantness of pre-trial detention.

Legal aid, for example, will, other things equal, increase the

---

[1] G. Williams, 'Questioning by Police: Some Practical Considerations', *Criminal Law Review*, 1960, pp. 325-46.

criminal court's case-load. The rules of evidence will also affect both the prevalence of plea bargains and the size of the sentence reduction. In England the procedural rules which exclude certain types of evidence are much weaker than in the United States. Other things equal, this will lead to a higher probability of conviction of defendants in England and, in turn, a lower reduction in sentence in any plea bargain. Thus the disparity between the sentences imposed on those who plead guilty in England and those who insist on a trial will be lower than in jurisdictions with strong exclusionary rules of evidence. Also, if criminal investigation and prosecution are the responsibility of a single law enforcement agency, there will be a predictable effect on the number of cases disposed of by trial. Other things equal, the cost-saving of a pre-trial settlement is higher for an agency which must bear the costs of both investigation and prosecution. Once the case goes to trial, however, such an agency will be relatively more reluctant to dismiss it.

Risk Aversion

Cost-savings are not the only factor explaining the practice of plea bargaining. If both the accused and the prosecutor are risk averse, they may agree to exchange a lighter sentence for a plea of guilty to avoid the uncertainty of trial. The plea bargain can also be used by the prosecutor to screen the guilty from the innocent. A guilty person is much more likely to plead his guilt in return for a lighter sentence, other things equal, than an innocent one. Thus the practice can be seen as an 'efficient' way of sorting the guilty from the innocent. But this will be true only if all those accused are equally risk-averse. If those accused of crimes but who are innocent are more risk-averse than those who are guilty, they may plead guilty simply to avoid the uncertain prospect of a heavier penalty.

Moreover, prosecutors may engage in 'overcharging' as a way of encouraging defendants to plead guilty. They may bring a number of unjustified charges in order to encourage the accused to believe that the sentence discount that is being offered is large and generous. This effectively imposes a surcharge on going to court and may result in those preferring a trial receiving a stiffer sentence to deter trials rather than crimes; that is, the innocent 'crowd out' the guilty with more and more resources spent on trying innocent people. In Britain there is no direct evidence on the validity of these conjectures. Baldwin and McConville's controversial study of plea bargaining in England found that a significant proportion of their sample who alleged they were innocent had pleaded guilty but that there was no evidence of 'overcharging'.[1]

The widespread use of the plea bargain has another effect on the procedures of criminal law. A principle of Anglo-American criminal law is that the guilt of the accused must be proved 'beyond reasonable doubt'. The plea bargain compromises this principle. It has the effect of reducing the standard of proof required to gain a conviction. This is because the prosecutor is able to trade doubt and poor evidence about the accused's guilt for a lower sentence.

From this brief discussion it can be seen that examining a legal phenomenon in an economic framework can help identify the consequences of a procedural practice (in this case, a *sub rosa* one denied to exist) on the operation of the law in everyday practice.

Defining Legal Terms

The most novel role the economist can adopt is that of *economic rhetorician*. This is the use of economics to give greater clarity or an alternative definition to legal terms. Interestingly, most of the practitioners of this application of economics have been lawyers, thus providing a rare example where those colonised have become the imperialists.

It may seem an odd, not to say arrogant, contention to suggest that an economist is required to (re)-interpret the words of judges before they can be understood. But the reason why it is a plausible endeavour is that English judges rarely state general principles of law. The common law, which is the customary law of the land evolved through decisions of judges in cases over centuries, is not based on a set of rules or a code. It is based on decisions in specific cases which are used as precedents for deciding subsequent cases. The common law has been described as a system of law which places a particular value on dissension, obscurity and the tentative character of judicial utterances so 'that uniquely authentic statements of the rule ... cannot be made'.[2] Thus, one of the principal activities of lawyers is to shift and categorise cases in order to distil the 'rules' of law. It is this

[1] Baldwin and McConville, *op. cit.*

[2] B. Simpson, 'The Common Law and Legal Theory', in W. Twining (ed.), *Legal Theory and Common Law*, Oxford: Basil Blackwell, 1986, p. 17.

'murkiness' of the common law which has permitted economics to be used to suggest new definitions for key legal concepts.[1]

Economists and lawyers have analysed legal doctrines and have shown many to have an economic definition. Legal doctrines such as 'reasonableness', 'remoteness', 'standard of care', 'foreseeability', 'privity' and 'causation' have all been analysed.[2]

Negligence

The economic analysis of negligence provides the starting point for much of the new economics of law. The law of negligence governs whether or not victims of harms, such as road accidents or medical negligence, should be compensated by those who injure them. Under the common law, in most accident situations the injurer is held liable only if he or she has failed to exercise sufficient care—that is, acted negligently or has been at 'fault'. The most famous statement of negligence in English (and Scottish) law is contained in Lord Atkin's *dicta* in *Donoghue v. Stevenson*:

> 'You must not injure your neighbour, and the lawyers' question: Who is my neighbour? receives a restricted reply. You must take reasonable care to avoid acts or omissions which you can reasonably foresee would injure your neighbour. Who then, in law, is my neighbour? The answer seems to be persons who are so closely and directly affected by my act that I ought reasonably to have them in contemplation as being so affected when I am directing my mind to the acts and omissions.'[3]

As stated, this judicial test is extremely vague. Its constituent parts are supplied by the decision of judges in specific cases over time. Yet the linguistic formulations used by judges such as 'duty of care', 'reasonable foreseeability', 'proximity', and 'reasonable care' have a chameleon-like quality. They are frequently used interchangeably, confusing lawyer and layman alike. The result is that the general principles of English common law are open-ended. The cases applying the law supply a patchwork of

---

[1] For a discussion of this use of economics, C. G. Veljanovski, 'Legal Theory, Economic Analysis and the Law of Torts', in Twining, *ibid.*, Ch. 12.

[2] For recent syntheses of this literature in tort, S. Shavell, *Economic Analysis of Accident Law*, Cambridge, Mass.: Harvard University Press, 1987; W. M. Landes and R. A. Posner, *The Economic Structure of Tort Law*, Cambridge, Mass.: Harvard University Press, 1987.

[3] *Donoghue v. Stevenson* (1932), A.C. 562, at p. 58.

decisions where the underlying logic, if any, is not self-evident.

The economist approaches the analysis of legal doctrine in a way entirely alien to that of the lawyer. He uses concepts such as choice, trade-offs, incentive effects, marginal analysis, externalities, and the cheapest cost avoider, as the basis for each discussion of a doctrine or case. The law is treated functionally in terms of distinctions between care and activity levels, alternative and joint care, accidents between strangers and those occurring in situations where the parties have a pre-existing 'exchange' relationship. The lawyer is offered an entirely new vocabulary to redefine legal terms.

The Hand Test

Consider the way the courts determine the legal standard of care in negligence. The typical situation is that A (the defendant) has harmed B (the plaintiff) by some action resulting from lack of care on A's (and frequently B's) part. A drives carelessly, changing lanes and crashing into another vehicle, or a doctor leaves a pair of forceps in B's body during an operation. An economist would assign the loss resulting from an accident to the party or parties most able to avoid it. The decision as to who should bear the loss would be made on the basis of the costs of avoidance to the plaintiff and defendant compared with the expected damages. Indeed, a US court decision by Judge Learned Hand explicitly formulates the standard of care in these terms. According to the 'Hand Test', the defendant's culpability is determined by balancing 'the burden of adequate precautions' (B) against 'the likelihood of an accident' (P) multiplied by the gravity of the harm should the accident occur (L).[1] If the cost of avoiding the accident exceeds the expected harm, then avoidance would increase costs. The Hand Test imposes liability on the defendant only if it can be established that accident avoidance is the cheapest solution (see Box 2). It mirrors closely the earlier discussion of the economics of safety (pp. 44-46).

The Hand Test is no judicial aberration. It encapsulates the main considerations used by the courts in England and other Commonwealth countries, and most casebooks and texts use the three factors (risk, precautions and gravity) to organise their

---

[1] *United States v. Carroll Towing Co.*, 159 F. 2d. 169, 173 (2d Cir.), 1947.

BOX 2

Economic Application of the Hand Test

In *United States v. Carroll Towing Co.*, 159 F.2d 169 (2d Cir. 1947), the question was presented whether it was negligent for the Conners Company, the owner of a barge, to leave it unattended for several hours in a busy harbour. While unattended, the barge broke away from its moorings and collided with another ship. Judge Learned Hand stated for the court (at page 173):

'There is no general rule to determine when the absence of a bargee or other attendant will make the owner of the barge liable for injuries to other vessels if she breaks away from her moorings . . . It becomes apparent why there can be no such general rule, when we consider the grounds for such a liability. Since there are occasions when every vessel will break from her moorings, and since, if she does, she becomes a menace to those about her, the owner's duty, as in other similar situations, to provide against resulting injuries is a function of three variables: (1) The probability that she will break away; (2) the gravity of the resulting injury, if she does; (3) the burden of adequate precautions. Possibly it serves to bring this notion into relief to state it in algebraic terms: if the probability be called P; the injury L; and the burden B; liability depends upon whether B is less than L multiplied by P: i.e., whether $B < PL$. . . . In the case at bar the bargee left at five o'clock on the afternoon of January 3rd, and the flotilla broke away at about two o'clock in the afternoon of the following day, twenty-one hours afterwards. The bargee had been away all the time, and we hold that his fabricated story was affirmative evidence that he had no excuse for his absence. At the locus in quo— especially during the short January days and in the full tide of war

discussion of the cases.[1] The Hand formula can be regarded as a convenient summary of the factors relevant to determining whether the defendant has breached his duty to take reasonable care for the protection of others. To illustrate this point, consider some of the classic cases familiar to all English law students.

---

[1] Hand-like statements of the breach of duty test can be found in *Mackintosh v. Mackintosh* 2 M. 1357 (1864); *Ryan v. Fisher* (1976) 51 ALJR 125; *Morris v. West Hartlepool Steam Navigation Co.* (1956) HL 574/5. A number of casebooks and texts covering the principal common law jurisdictions are organised around the Hand formula: B. Hepple and M. Matthews, *Tort – Cases and Materials*, London: Butterworth, 2nd edn., 1980, Ch. 4; R. A. Posner, *Tort Law – Cases and Economic Analysis*, Boston: Little Brown, 1984; Linden, *Canadian Tort Law*, Toronto: Caswell, 1977, pp. 80-90; H. Luntz *et al.*, *Torts: Cases and Commentary*, Sydney: Law Book Co., 1980, Ch. 3.

activity—barges were being constantly 'drilled' in and out. Certainly it was not beyond reasonable expectation that, with the inevitable haste and bustle, the work might not be done with adequate care. In such circumstances we hold—and it is all that we do hold—that it was a fair requirement that the Conners Company should have a bargee aboard (unless he had some excuse for his absence), during the working hours of daylight.'

By redefinition of two terms in the Hand formula it is easy to bring out its economic character. B, the burden of precautions, is the cost of avoiding the accident, while L, the loss if the accident occurs, is the cost of the accident itself. P times L (P x L)—the cost of the accident if it occurs, multiplied (or, as is sometimes said, 'discounted') by the probability that the accident will occur—is what an economist would call the 'expected cost' of the accident. Expected cost is most easily understood as the average cost that will be incurred over a period of time long enough for the predicted number of accidents to be the actual number.

For example, if the probability that a certain type of accident will occur is ·001 (one in a thousand) and the accident cost if it does occur is $10,000, the expected accident cost is $10 ($10,000 x ·001); and this is equivalent to saying that if we observe the activity that gives rise to this type of accident for a long enough period of time we will observe an average accident cost of $10. Suppose the activity in question is automobile trips from point A to point B. If there are 100,000 trips, there will be 100 accidents, assuming that our probability of ·001 was correct. The total cost of the 100 accidents will be $1 million ($10,000 x 100). The average cost, which is simply the total cost ($1 million) divided by the total number of trips (100,000), will be $10. This is the same as the expected cost.

Source: R. A. Posner, *Tort Law—Cases and Economic Analysis*, Boston: Little-Brown, 1982, p. 1.

Under the Hand Test the defendant is more likely to be found in breach of his duty if the costs of care are low, the risks of injury high, and the severity of the injuries, should an accident occur, are high. It is the interplay of these three factors that is important to the decision whether the defendant has breached his duty of care. As we shall see, all these factors are important in law.

The likelihood of injury (L) is a relevant factor in determining whether the risk created by the defendant is unreasonable. In *Fardon v. Harcourt-Rivington*[1] Lord Dunedin stated that 'people must guard against reasonable probabilities, but they are not bound to guard against fantastic possibilities'.

[1] [1932] 146 L.T. 391.

In *Bolton v. Stone*[1] a batsman hit a ball over a fence onto an adjoining highway, injuring the plaintiff. In the 90-year period over which cricket had been played on the field no-one had ever been injured, and in the previous 30 years the ball had been hit over the fence only six times. The House of Lords found the defendant not liable because the chance of injury 'was very small'. Lord Reid applied the following test:

'whether the risk of damage to a person on the road was so small that a reasonable man . . ., considering the matter from the view of safety, would have thought it right to refrain from taking steps to prevent the danger'.

In economic terms the risk of injury was very small so that the damage was discounted very heavily (i.e. P x L is very low). Also, the facts in the case show that the fence was already 29 feet high (it was a 12-foot fence built on a 17-foot rise) so that the costs of avoiding such an accident were bound to be very high (hence B is considerably greater than P x L).

In *Haley v. London Electricity Board*[2] the factors in the Hand equation are discussed more fully. The defendant (the LEB) was excavating a pavement and as a precaution placed a punner[3] at one end of the excavation on the completion of the day's work. The plaintiff, who was blind and could avoid ordinary obstacles only with the aid of a white stick, missed the punner and tripped. As a result he hit his head and became deaf. In this case the defendant alleged that the chance of a blind man coming along the road that day was small and that therefore it was not reasonable to expect him to take precautions. Lord Reid did not agree. Evidence was presented that one in 500 people in London at the time were blind. He went on to consider the costs of taking adequate precautions. Padded lamp-posts, for example, were not justified in view of the risks. But he continued:

'A moment's reflection . . . shows that a low obstacle in an unusual place is a grave danger: on the other hand, it is clear that quite a light fence some two feet high is adequate warning. There would be no difficulty in providing such a fence here.'

(The reason why such a fence was not provided by the LEB was that it arrived late.)

The standard of care required of the defendant will tend to

[1] [1951] 1 All ER 1078.   [2] [1964] 3 All ER 185.

[3] A tool for ramming earth around a post to make it firm.

rise with the magnitude of the harm. In *Paris v. Stepney Borough Council*[1] a one-eyed man was blinded when a chip of metal lodged in his good eye. The plaintiff argued that his employer was negligent in failing to supply him with goggles even though these were not usually provided to employees. The court held that, although it would not have been negligent not to provide full-sighted employees with goggles, it was in this case because the consequences were more serious. In Lord Morton's judgement he stated that 'the more serious the damage which will happen if an accident occurs, the more thorough are the precautions which employers must take'. He also made it clear that the right-hand side of the Hand Test (P x L) is relevant:

'In considering generally the precautions that the employer ought to take for the protection of his workmen it must, in my view, be right to take into account both elements, the likelihood of an accident happening and the gravity of the consequences.'

The cost of reducing risk is explicitly referred to in other cases. In *Watt v. Hertfordshire County Council*[2] Lord Denning stated that in measuring due care one must balance the risk against the measures necessary to eliminate it. If the costs of precautions are minimal, liability is more likely to follow. In the Australian case, *Mercer v. Commissioner for Road Transport and Tramways*,[3] the driver of a tram collapsed at the controls and, despite the efforts of the conductor to stop it with the hand brakes, a collision resulted. The plaintiff alleged that a 'dead man's handle' which automatically stops a tram if released would have avoided the accident. The court held that, in terms of the risk that would be avoided, the costs would be disproportionate.

Sometimes the courts will excuse the defendant's conduct if it has a high 'social utility'. In *Daborn v. Bath Tramways Motor Co. Ltd. and T. Smithey*[4] the plaintiff was driving a left-hand drive ambulance. The plaintiff gave a signal but collided with a bus. Here several issues were discussed. Counsel for the defendants argued that 'the driver of such a car should, before executing a turn, stop his car, move to the right-hand seat and look backwards to see if another car was attempting to overtake him and then start up again'. Lord Asquith was satisfied both that this procedure would involve possible delay and that it might be

1 [1951] 1 All ER 42.   2 [1954] 2 All ER 368, 371.
3 [1937] 56 CLR 580.   4 [1946] 2 All ER 333 (CA).

ineffective. The court considered another cost. It was a time of national emergency requiring all transport resources to be employed. The risk could have been eliminated by forbidding such vehicles to be used. But, as the judge pointed out, this cost must be weighed against the reduction in risk.

Daborn is an application of the opportunity cost concept. In *Daborn* the cost of prohibiting left-hand drive ambulances was the forgone social benefits. And the opportunity cost of forbearing from using these ambulances (B in terms of the Hand formulation) had to be compared with the reduction in (total) expected losses from using them.

Formal Economic Model of Negligence

The Hand Test is not an entirely accurate representation of the economics of negligence nor the way the courts decide negligence. Care is not an on/off situation. It is a *continuum* of more or less care or actions which could avoid the accident. The Hand formula is misleading on this account. As stated it gave the impression that greater care would avoid the victim's loss completely. While this may be true in some cases, it is generally not so. From an economic viewpoint optimal care is defined as a situation where an additional £1 spent on safety decreases expected loss by £1—that is, actual loss discounted by the *reduction* in the likelihood of the accident occurring (point C* in Figure 2). That is to say, we make comparisons with marginal or incremental costs, not total costs and expected losses.

Consider the following example. Suppose that my house is on a particularly sharp bend on the road so that visitors must negotiate an acute angle to turn into my drive. A number of visitors have damaged their cars entering my drive. Assume that the risk of damage is one in 10 and that damage to vehicles averages to about £100. If I move one of the fence posts I can reduce the likelihood that future visitors will damage their cars from one in 10 to one in 20. Assume that it costs me only £2 to move the post. Should I move it and, if I do not, should I be found negligent? The answer is 'yes'. It costs me £2 to move the post but, as a result, I save my visitors 5 per cent of £100 = £5. Thus, in determining whether the plaintiff has been negligent, we must compare the costs of the actions which could have been taken against the reduction in the risks that these bring about. That is, the comparison is between the *marginal* costs of greater care and the *marginal* reduction in expected losses. If marginal

[70]

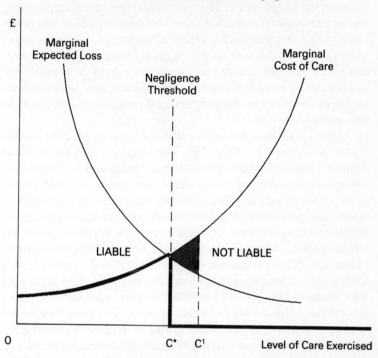

Figure 2:
The Way an Economist Sees Negligence

safety costs are less than marginal expected loss, more care is economically efficient, and the defendant should be held liable (in Figure 2 care less than C*). If the next unit of care costs £2 but avoids only £1 of damage, excessive precautions have been taken and no damages should be awarded.

In practice, courts do decide negligence cases in this way, albeit less formally and rigorously. Even though the judge makes binary choices (guilty/not guilty), the grounds upon which judges decide negligence are incremental. The adversarial style of common law adjudication forces the lawyer and judge to think not in terms of absolutes but in terms of incremental changes. The judge determines whether or not the defendant has acted unreasonably. But this disguises the way the courts determine fault and how lawyers present their clients' cases. To establish fault the plaintiff has to persuade the judge that on the balance of probabilities the defendant did not act with reasonable care. The plaintiff will enumerate actions which, had the

[71]

defendant taken them, would have avoided the accident. The defendant will counter with reasons why this would not have reduced the likelihood of harm or would have been impractical, too expensive and unreasonable. The *basis* on which the judge decides and the process by which he arrives at this decision are very similar to the way in which an economist would *approach* the problem. The courts, in effect, engage in a 'cost-benefit' analysis. As Posner has recently emphasised, cost-benefit analysis 'at least describes the judgemental process' of the courts in tort cases.[1]

A good judicial application of marginal cost analysis can be found in *Latimer v. AEC Ltd.* The respondent's factory was flooded by an unusually heavy thunderstorm and a collection of water and oil collected on the floor. Sawdust was spread on the floor but there was insufficient to deal with the (large) quantity of water. The court held that there was enough sawdust to meet any situation that could have been foreseen. The appellant, who was working on the night shift, was injured when he slipped on a wet, oily patch, crushing his leg, whilst trying to load a barrel onto a trolley. This case illustrates nicely the fact that the courts take into account the costs of additional care and balance them against the incremental reduction in risks. The issue before the court was whether a 'reasonably prudent employer would have closed down the factory rather than allow his employees to run the risks involved in continuing work'. Lord Tucker decided the danger was not such as to require the factory to close. In economic terms Lord Tucker was comparing the *additional costs* of closedown against the incremental reduction of the risks of injury to workers. In terms of Figure 2 the court felt that the employer was at C* (the economically efficient level of care). To require the shutdown of the factory (care level C¹) would have imposed a cost burden on the employer not fully offset by the gain to workers (the excess cost is the shaded area).

[1] R. A. Posner, 'Wealth Maximisation and Judicial Decision-Making', *International Review of Law and Economics*, Vol. 131, 1984, p. 134.

VI. REGULATION

The study of regulation has been woefully neglected by UK economists. Any theory and most empirical work is imported from the USA, and some of the critical thinking about the design of regulatory frameworks has been the result of 'privatised research'—economists employed as advisers to government or as consultants to industry. The innovation has been in policy, with economic research lagging behind in responding to government proposals rather than providing a solid base for efficient regulatory frameworks. Regulation is growing rapidly in the UK. During the Thatcher decade supply-side reforms have led to the increasing use of regulation administered by semi-autonomous public bodies as a technique of legal control.[1] Regulation takes the form of statute, subordinate legislation and other administrative devices such as guidance notes, Ministerial orders, licensing procedures and decisions, and a host of opaque activities of government.

British economists have been confused about regulation—exhibiting a schizophrenia—regulation is good in theory, yet in practice displays a bewildering complexity and inefficiency not explained by their 'market failure' theory of good regulation.

In this section a jaundiced view of regulation is offered. It is argued that regulation invariably achieves modest results at significant costs. The principal reason is that it is frequently not designed to be efficient but to favour certain sections of industry or politically influential groups.

Models of Regulation

A recent survey of regulatory reform in Britain by two economists concluded:

'The primary rationale for regulation . . . is to remedy various kinds of market failure.'[2]

---

[1] For a discussion of this development, C. G. Veljanovski, *Selling the State – Privatisation in Britain*, London: Weidenfeld & Nicolson, 1988; also Veljanovski (ed.), *Privatisation and Competition – A Market Prospectus*, London: IEA, 1989.

[2] J. Kay and J. Vickers, 'Regulatory Reform in Britain', *Economic Policy*, Vol. 7, 1988, p. 301.

It listed three types of market failure: external costs, market power and inadequate information. The authors went on to observe:

'The normal pattern is that market failure provides the rationale for the introduction of regulation, but the scope of regulation is then extended to a wide range of matters which are the subject of general or sectional interests, regardless of whether there is any element of market failure or not.'[1]

The survey was interesting in several respects. First, it offered *no* evidence that market failure was or is the predominant rationale for actual regulations. Second, the survey drew on a narrow literature on regulation to support its claim and to 'explain' regulation. For example, the authors failed to cite the important work of Nobel Laureates George Stigler[2] and James Buchanan, who have developed an economic theory directly at odds with the claim that market failure is the primary and most important explanation of regulation. The Stigler theory, discussed briefly in Section II (above, p. 20), suggests that regulation is motivated by and panders to sectional interests from its inception and not as an afterthought. Finally, few economists who have studied regulation would concur with the conclusions of these authors. They fail accurately to reflect the emerging consensus of US economists in the 1970s, of both major political persuasions, that regulation has generally 'failed'. Consider the following evaluations of the US experience by two respected scholars in the field. Professor Roger Noll of Stanford University:

'By the early 1970s the overwhelming majority of economists had reached consensus on two points. First, economic regulation did not succeed in protecting consumers against monopolies, and indeed often served to create monopolies out of workably competitive industries or to protect monopolies against new firms seeking to challenge their position. Second, in circumstances where market failures were of enduring importance (such as environmental protection), traditional standard-setting regulation was usually a far less effective remedy than the use of markets and incentives (such as emissions taxes or tradable emissions permits).'[3]

---

[1] *Ibid.*, p. 334. See also S. Breyer and P. W. MacAvoy, 'Regulation and Deregulation', in *The New Palgrave Dictionary of Economics*, London: Macmillan, 1987, pp. 128-37.

[2] G. J. Stigler, 'The Theory of Economic Regulation', *Bell Journal of Economics & Management Science*, 1971, p. 241; R. A. Posner, 'Theories of Economic Regulation', *Bell Journal of Economics & Management Science*, 1974, p. 335.

[3] R. G. Noll, 'Regulation After Reagan', *Regulation*, No. 3, 1988, p. 20.

Or Professor George Stigler's more strident conclusion:

'The paramount role traditionally assigned by economists to government regulation was to correct the failures of the private market (the unconsidered effects of behaviour on outsiders), but in fact the premier role of modern regulation is to redistribute income.'[1]

Regulatory Failure

Regulation has a dismal record because of the forces in the political market-place and the choice of inappropriate techniques of regulation.

The Thatcher Government could be supposed to have adopted an economically rational programme of regulatory reform. Its White Papers are full of concern about the need to avoid the excesses of so-called 'US-style regulation'—cost-plus litigious regulation which places excessive burdens on industry and the consumer. The British approach, in contrast, is based on economic rationality, simplicity and the all-round pragmatism characteristic of the English mind which avoids the excesses of other governments. Yet this description is merely a civilised way of saying that the process has been *ad hoc*, has lacked a coherent strategy, and has been guided too often by short-term considerations and administrative convenience.

One does not need to burrow into the intricacies of economic analysis to unearth stark examples of regulatory failure. Consider the following short list drawn from the late 1980s and the product of a Government committed to regulatory reform and economic rationalism:

1. There has been major confusion surrounding new investor protection laws. The Securities and Investment Board (SIB), the principal regulatory agency, adopted a legalistic, inflexible and incoherent approach to its regulatory responsibilities, sparking a crisis in the City and Whitehall, the 'sacking' of its Chairman, the re-writing of the SIB's rulebook, and the repeal of key sections of the new Financial Services Act in 1988. The past Chairman of the Securities and Investment Board, Sir Kenneth Berrill, was often heard to claim that the new legal framework for investor protection would protect the ordinary small investor—the Aunt Agathas of Britain. But there was no evidence of this, nor was there a

[1] G. J. Stigler (ed.), *Chicago Studies in Political Economy*, Chicago: University of Chicago Press, 1988, p. xii.

preparedness on the part of the regulators to examine critically the techniques of intervention to determine their effectiveness.[1]

2. The Barlow Clowes affair, which initiated the Government's concern over the adequacy of investor protection laws, demonstrated that bureaucracies can be inefficient. In 1989 the Government made an *ex gratia* payment to investors in Barlow Clowes of £100 million after the Ombudsman identified 'significant maladministration' by the Department of Trade and Industry.[2] The failure of the DTI to deal with other regulatory offences has now become a matter of general knowledge.

3. MacDonald Wheeler was an investment company authorised by a regulatory body. It was in fact managed by a twice-declared bankrupt who absconded with his clients' money. Investors were lulled into a false sense of security because the firm's letterhead stated that it was authorised by NASDIM, the then regulatory authority. Reliance on regulation is no guarantee that the investor will be protected from evident sources of wrongdoing. The regulatory body is now being sued for negligence.

4. The common carrier provisions of the Oil & Gas Enterprise Act 1982, the Energy Act 1983 and the Gas Act 1986, permit third parties to use the transmission system of either British Gas or the now defunct Central Electricity Generating Board (CEGB). All these pieces of legislation did not encourage competition because of the failure to provide adequate safeguards against monopoly abuse by British Gas and the CEGB.[3]

5. The Independent Broadcasting Authority (IBA), which regulates commercial television and radio in the UK, has a statutory duty to monitor the Independent Television (ITV) contractors' finances to ensure against excessive expenditure which would reduce their profits and hence the tax yield to the Treasury. The IBA has never reported excessive expendi-

[1] A. Seldon (ed.), *Financial Regulation – or Over-regulation?*, IEA Readings No. 27, London: Institute of Economic Affairs, 1988.

[2] Ombudsman, *The Barlow Clowes Affair*, London: HMSO, 1989.

[3] See C. Veljanovski (ed.), *Privatisation and Competition*, *op. cit.*, Chap. 1.

ture. Yet the Peacock Report[1] drew attention to this aspect of ITV's advertising monopoly and the ITV companies now admit that costs had risen over the years to an unacceptable level. The Public Accounts Committee expressed concern that neither the Home Office nor the IBA 'had *any* well-developed and quantified means of determining ... the efficiency of programme contractors ...'.[2] In short, both the Government and the regulatory bureaucracy had failed to carry out their statutory duty. A private sector company failing to audit its accounts properly would be subject to criminal prosecution and negligence action by its shareholders. The taxpayer has no such remedies.

These are illustrations of regulatory failure. A major reason for this is that the form of regulation selected and the incentives operating on those charged with administering and enforcing these regulations are inadequate.

Minimum Wage – Inappropriate Technique

The earlier discussion of housing legislation provided an example of the perverse effects of law. Consider the example of labour legislation. This is often presented as a method of improving the welfare of workers and ensuring their safety. But by interfering with prices in the economy such legislation distorts the allocation of resources and ends up disadvantaging the very workers it seeks to assist. It could be argued, in the manner of Kay and Vickers, that this is an unfortunate side-effect that had not been anticipated. But this is far-fetched, for it asserts that the persistence of inefficient regulation is the outcome of uncorrected mistakes, ignorance and errors. As Professor Stigler has commented, if this is the economist's approach to regulation, then a 'theory of errors' is required to gain any understanding of the regulatory process.

Consider the effects of minimum wage legislation. The belief underlying such legislation is that, by raising wages, lower-paid workers can be made better off. The European Commission's proposals for a 'Social Charter' seek to raise wages to a 'decent level'. The immediate effects of such a proposal are to increase the take-home pay of those benefiting from the legislation. But this also increases the employers' wage bill and the price of

[1] *Report of the Committee on Financing the BBC*, Cmnd. 9824, London: HMSO, 1986.

[2] Committee of Public Accounts, *Independent Broadcasting Authority: Additional payments by programme Contractors*, Cm. 317, London: HMSO, 1988.

labour. The laws of supply and demand will quickly react to the now more expensive low-productivity labour. Employers will find that with higher labour costs, their products are less competitive or even uncompetitive with imports or less labour-intensive substitute products. They will sack less productive workers and not hire those workers with poor skills. Unemployment will increase.[1] Moreover, if labour costs persist at higher than market-determined levels because of the law, employers will begin substituting capital for labour (instead of having several people sweeping the warehouse or loading lorries, vacuum cleaners and forklift trucks will be used), and where this cannot be done, prices will rise and output contract. The net result of the legislation is higher unemployment, lower output and higher prices for the products of those industries affected.

These effects will not be spread uniformly among firms, industries and regions. Those firms which rely on cheap labour and are relatively labour intensive will suffer most. Those regions which have a large number of labour-intensive industries and rely on products produced by low-skill labour will suffer relatively more than others. Those groups of workers which are itinerant, unreliable and/or casual will find it more difficult to secure jobs on terms which they find attractive.

This will have significant redistributive effects. Regulation raises the costs of some firms and industries more than others. This places them at a competitive disadvantage, causing major changes in employment and production. There will, in short, be significant gainers and losers from minimum wage legislation in addition to the workers initially affected. In the European Community, the Social Charter can be expected adversely to affect the Southern member-states and benefit those in the North which are already high-wage economies.

If regulation has these predictable effects which arise from raising competitors' costs, herein lies a theory of regulation. As Stigler contends, regulation fits into a logical pattern if one examines closely who are the gainers and losers rather than seeing it simply as a remedy for market failure.

Safety Regulation as a Barrier to Competition
Industrial safety legislation fits this pattern. The market-failure

---

[1] For some estimates of these effects, P. Minford and P. Ashton, 'The Effects in the UK of EEC Wage Proposals in the Social Charter—a Note', *Liverpool Quarterly Economic Bulletin*, Vol. 10, No. 4, December 1989.

approach interprets industrial safety regulation as a device to deal with the inability of the labour market to provide adequate levels of worker safety. Yet empirical research often fails to find any significant improvement in safety arising from such laws but does find that they increase industry costs substantially. A partial explanation lies in the redistributive effects of the type of industrial safety laws which are implemented. Typically they impose technical and legalistic standards which the employer must observe and which focus on increasing safety inputs rather than deterring accidents. For example, they require the employer to make capital expenditures such as purchasing machines with guards. This has the effect of raising the cost of capital whilst leaving labour relatively unregulated despite the fact that studies show that most accidents are the result either of worker carelessness or a combination of employer and worker carelessness. This benefits labour—safety legislation of this type taxes capital and leaves labour relatively unconstrained.

But industrial safety regulation has other indirect effects. Clearly, if the regulation is stringent and vigorously enforced it raises a firm's costs and makes entry into the industry more difficult for the smaller firm. If firms have different costs of complying, either due to their size or location, then regulation will have a more pronounced impact on some firms. A number of empirical studies have confirmed this analysis. The study of US industrial safety and environmental regulation by Bartel and Thomas[1] found that it had the effect of raising the profits of industries with a high proportion of their workers in large firms or in the 'frost belt', while those industries with a large number of small firms or in the 'sun belt' lost profits. This mirrors the predictions above of the European Commission's proposals for a 'decent wage'. It confers a competitive advantage on some firms by imposing higher costs on others. In short, regulation raises barriers to entry and reduces competitive pressures in industry.

Economics of Legal Rules

A major reason for the perverse effect of much regulation is the legalistic techniques which are employed. Here I briefly examine (a) the way economics can assist in framing legal rules which take into account costs and incentive effects, and (b) why legalistic

---

[1] A. P. Bartel and L. C. Thomas, 'Predation through Regulation: The Wage and Profit Effects of the Occupational Safety and Health Administration and the Environmental Protection Agency', *Journal of Law and Economics*, Vol. 30, 1987, pp. 239-65.

standards raise costs but do not necessarily improve the welfare of those protected.

If regulation is to be effective it must be framed with attention to costs and the adaptive responses of those regulated. The Thatcher Government has attempted this by implementing the Compliance Cost Assessment (CCA) system which requires all central government departments to identify the costs of each proposed regulation. This has not been successful. The procedure lacked political support and a coherent vision of the objectives to be achieved. This manifested itself in a failure by government departments to cost regulations adequately or to use cost-benefit techniques to select the most effective regulation. Rather, economics was bastardised to rationalise a department's preferred legalistic regulation.

The efficiency of any system of legal rules requires a balancing of three principal costs:

o   the costs of designing and implementing legal standards (rule-making costs);

o   the costs of enforcing the standards (enforcement costs); and

o   the costs that they impose on the regulated industry (compliance costs).

An 'efficient' system of enforcement is one that minimises the sum of these three costs plus the social losses inflicted by regulatory offences.[1]

Under- and Over-inclusion

In practice laws are not cost-effective in this sense. Specifically the law can be under- or over-inclusive. It can be under-inclusive because many socially undesirable activities and practices are left unregulated. Those activities that are regulated are often subject to over-inclusive laws which prevent or deter activities thought to be socially desirable by setting too stringent standards, compelling practices that are excessively costly and/or ineffective. A regulation is over-inclusive when the marginal avoided social or external losses from complying with a standard are less than the sum of compliance and enforcement costs.

An example will serve to illustrate the idea. In the UK the speed limit in an urban area is 30 mph. In general this rule is a

---

[1] I. Ehrlich and R. A. Posner, 'An Economic Analysis of Legal Rule-making', *Journal of Legal Studies*, Vol. 3, 1974, pp. 257-86.

rough-and-ready way of ensuring adequate road safety. But in many specific instances it is not. The expectant father bundles his wife about to give birth into the family car and speeds to the local hospital. A policeman sees the speeding vehicle and stops it. Common sense tells us that rigidly enforcing the law in this case will do more harm than good—the rule is over-inclusive. Consider another example. Trade unions frequently threaten to 'work to rule'. This is regarded as a real threat which can bring the firm to a halt.

Ignoring for the moment the claim made above that rules may not be intended to achieve efficiency, some degree of over-inclusion will inevitably arise from cost and information factors which make it impossible to devise the most effective intervention. For a regulation to be cost-effective, the standard-setting body (whether it be Parliament or a government department) must possess considerable information on the technological and economic conditions surrounding abatement and the degree of harm caused by hazards. The cost of collecting and processing this information will tend to limit the extent to which standards match the least-cost method of abatement. These information and implementation costs will tend to be greater the more complex, diverse, and/or extensive the activity that is being controlled. In addition, the regulators will be involved in consultation with the regulated and interested parties, such as trade unions, giving rise to another set of costs (negotiation and consultation costs) and delay in the enactment of regulations.

The combination of these factors will lead to a regulatory framework that is often poorly matched to the cost-effective means of achieving regulatory objectives. Many breaches of the law will be technical ones that have very little to do with encouraging desirable behaviour or that achieve improvements at disproportionate cost. The problem of over-inclusion thus arises and will be accentuated over time, especially when changes in technology and economic conditions are rapid. As stated in the Robens Report, 'obsolescence is a chronic disease of the statutory safety provision'.[1]

The Effects of Over-inclusion

It is specifically because of over-inclusion that legalistic methods of regulation are chosen. They regulate in a way that purports to

[1] Robens Report, *Committee on Safety and Health at Work*, Cmnd. 5034, London: HMSO, 1972, para. 29.

achieve the goals of the law but in practice favours some at the expense of others.

As already mentioned, much industrial safety legislation focusses on safety rather than on accidents. The employer is required to fit guards to machines or conform to certain safety practices under the threat of criminal prosecution. These control safety inputs rather than penalise the harm—accidents. Professor Robert Smith summarises the economist's objections to this approach:

> 'First, standards may bear no relationship to the hazards in a particular operation, yet compliance (at whatever the cost) is mandatory. Second, by requiring a certain set of safety inputs rather than by penalising an unwanted outcome, such as injuries, the standards approach does not encourage firms to seek other perhaps cheaper ways of reducing injuries. Third, the promulgated standards are so numerous and workplaces so diverse, that one must question how comprehensive or knowledgeable inspections can be.'[1]

It is also invariably the case that statutory regulations focus on those aspects of the problems which are easy to regulate rather than on the main causes of significant harms. For example, the Factory Act focusses disproportionately on machinery accidents despite the fact that many more accidents are the result of workers falling, slipping or handling objects.

It is relatively easy to envisage a situation where firms respond to intensified enforcement of ineffective regulation in a way that does not improve the position of consumers and workers. Consider the following situation. The law controls a number of safety inputs which are relatively ineffective in reducing workplace accidents. These are enforced vigorously. The firm responds by complying, thus raising its costs. But it also rationally adapts to these increased costs by relaxing other aspects of workplace safety which are not subject to regulation and may be more effective in reducing accidents. This adaptive response is graphically illustrated by a case unearthed by Kagan and Scholz[2] in their study of the enforcement of industrial safety regulation by the US Occupational Safety and Health Administration (OSHA). A steel company became embroiled in

---

[1] R. S. Smith, 'The Feasibility of an "Injury Tax" Approach to Occupational Safety', *Law and Contemporary Problems*, Vol. 38, 1974, p. 730.

[2] R. A. Kagan and J. T. Scholz, in K. Hawkins and J. M. Thomas (eds.), *Enforcing Regulation*, Boston: Kluwer-Nijhoff, 1984, Chap. 4.

disputes with OSHA, which during the 1970s adopted an aggressive enforcement policy. One of the firm's immediate responses to what it regarded as unreasonable persecution by OSHA was to sack its trained safety engineer who headed its accident-prevention programme and replace him with a lawyer. This outcome is a clear example where the response was to substitute one input (in this case to deal with regulation) for another more effective in reducing harm and improving worker welfare.

Thus under legalistic modes of regulation a situation can arise where increased enforcement leads to greater compliance and higher costs for some firms, but because firms have adapted to this constraint by relaxing other aspects of workplace safety, accidents do not fall and may even increase. The odd thing is that the regulator can claim success—after all, has not the level of enforcement and prosecutions increased and more firms complied with safety laws? Yet looking behind these official statistics, we see industries' costs rising and workers bewildered by the fact that there has been no appreciable increase in job safety.

A more graphic and well-documented example is seat-belt legislation. Road accidents are the result of the interaction of roads (their construction, topography, lighting and safety features), car design and use, and driver and pedestrian actions. As the roads are made safer there is a natural inclination for drivers to take more risks by driving faster and less carefully, and braking too late. They will substitute free publicly provided road safety for costly privately produced safety. In the economic literature this effect was first recognised by Sam Peltzman[1] in his work on the impact of mandatory seat-belt legislation in the USA. He argued that because seat belts reduced driver risks and injuries, drivers adjusted their behaviour by driving faster and with 'less care, thereby increasing the number of accidents, changing the type of accidents and raising total accident losses. This phenomenon has been identified independently by safety researchers as 'risk compensation'.

The Techniques of Intervention

The source of much regulatory ineffectiveness is the technique of legal control. The legal rule enforced by criminal or civil sanctions presupposes that the rule is framed to avoid perverse

1 S. Peltzman, 'The Effects of Automobile Safety Regulation', *Journal of Political Economy*, Vol. 83, 1975, p. 677.

incentive effects. Yet there are available other techniques of regulation which rely on economic incentives that deal directly with economic and social harms.

The first are fiscal devices which have become fashionable. This is to tax the polluter on the so-called 'polluter must pay' principle. By imposing a tax on pollution or injuries which approximates the uncompensated losses imposed on other individuals, the industry is left to decide whether clean-up is cost-effective and in what ways it can be undertaken.

Another device is the marketable permit. Here pollution permits are issued to existing industries up to the level of the desired cutback. The permits can then be traded. This creates a market in pollution in which firms which find it unprofitable to reduce the level of, say, toxic emissions, sell permits to other firms which can achieve reductions at low cost or which value the right to pollute very highly. In this way the desired reduction in pollution is achieved in the least costly way.

The most market-like response to pollution is to privatise scarce natural resource by assigning property rights to individuals. Consider the plight of the African elephant. The regulatory response is to have state-run National Parks and a militia which guns down or is gunned downed by poachers. The government can respond to increased poaching (which is a product of the world demand for ivory) by making the penalties for poaching draconian and burning any confiscated ivory. But this in the end only sends the market price of ivory soaring and increases the gains from poaching. An alternative response is to privatise the elephants. If elephant farms were permitted, normal economic forces would ensure that these precious beasts were not poached to extinction.

Conclusions

Examining regulation solely in terms of a response to market failure is a blind alley. Regulation can be a remedy for the failings of the market-place, but it is more often a substitute for markets designed to destroy competition and redistribute income from consumers, small firms and potential competitors towards larger firms.

On the basis of the mounting evidence on the performance of regulation, several generalisations can be made:

o Market failure and the theory of regulation it has spawned

[84]

does not explain actual regulation. Economists must explicitly take account of the fact that before a policy becomes effective, it suffers the ravages of the political and legal systems, two worlds populated by economic illiterates and self-interested individuals. If a camel is a horse designed by a committee, regulatory failure is the product of the political and legal worlds in collusion against the consumer and competitor.

o Both regulation and the market are imperfect. As Professor Fred Kahn has concluded after an illustrious career as an academic, intellectual entrepreneur and regulator:

'The verdict of the great majority of economists would, I believe, be that deregulation has been a success—bearing in mind ... that society's choices are always between or among imperfect systems, but that, wherever it seems likely to be effective, even imperfect competition is preferable to regulation. ...'[1]

The idea that markets work better than bureaucracy is one which is in the ascendancy. This was not always the case. But the truth that much regulation, whether old or new, fails is one that has not penetrated the work of most economists.

o One of the major deficiencies of regulation is the techniques used. These are predominantly legalistic common-and-control approaches rather than 'incentive regulation'. The use of market-like techniques of regulation such as taxes, property rights and marketable permits would lead to greater effectiveness.

o Very little research or knowledge exists on the relationship between actual regulation and its impact on those regulated and protected in the UK. It is invariably assumed by lawmakers that the law is faithfully adhered to and that what is assumed to be its effects are its effects. The dictum has been that 'regulation is costless; its effects good'. This dictum is most certainly wrong.

It is worth reiterating the main thrust of this section. It has been a criticism of economists for neglecting a subject vital to the function of the economy and its markets. Regulation is pervasive, especially when it is defined to embrace property rights and the legal framework which enables gains from trade in

[1] Alfred E. Kahn, *The Economics of Regulation: Principles and Institutions*, Cambridge, Mass.: MIT Press, 1988, p. xxiii.

the market-place. And it is here that the criticism turns squarely on economists for what can only be described as an intellectual failure of major proportions. If British economics was a product and its suppliers all members of the same for-profit partnership it would be facing insolvency because it failed to undertake the basic research on the major questions of industrial policy in the 1980s and equally failed to position itself to exploit the wealth this would have created. As the IEA's recent survey of economists[1] has clearly shown, the profession is not in a healthy state.

[1] M. Ricketts and E. Shoesmith, *British Economic Opinion: A Survey of a Thousand Economists*, Research Monograph 45, London: Institute of Economic Affairs, 1990.

VII. SUMMARY AND CONCLUSIONS

Summary

In this *Hobart Paper* I have sought to introduce the reader to a new application of economics. The economics of law is rapidly being transformed: from an esoteric academic pursuit it is beginning to challenge and extend the frontiers of industrial and economic policy. As the pace of privatisation and deregulation quickens and spreads across the world, increasingly vexing questions concerning institutional design must be addressed and answered. In the UK, lawyers, civil servants and economists have been slow to recognise this task so that policy has proceeded at breakneck speed without the benefit of serious analysis or proper guidance. The next several decades will prove a fertile playground as the deficiencies of regulation come to be recognised.

In the main body of this *Hobart Paper* the fundamental tenets of economics have been emphasised. Economics is concerned with choice and alternatives, and the forgone opportunities that surround individual and political decisions. At the core of economics is the assumption that individuals act purposively to select those alternatives in those quantities which maximise their welfare as perceived by them. It is this assumption that gives economics its explanatory power—the ability to anticipate better than other approaches the consequences of changes in the conditions of choice.

The theory of choice which underpins economics leads to a fundamentally different view of law which, while not alien to lawyers, is not central. As I have argued, economists perceive the law as a giant pricing machine. Its framework of duties, rights and obligations creates a system of constraints and penalties which alter the net benefits of different courses of action. In a crude way, the law prices and taxes individual human behaviour and therefore influences that behaviour.

The economics of law offers the prospect of a more rational and sensible way of devising regulation. Apart from the intellectual excitement generated by these different uses of economics, the ultimate value is the way they shed light on the operation of the economy and institutions. By a detailed study of law, legal institutions and organisations we can gain a better understanding of the way economies and industries function. Economic analysis can provide information on the effects, costs and benefits of different laws, thereby identifying the least restrictive and most effective way to implement regulation.

To the Lawyers and Regulators

Laws exist for a purpose—they are not an end in themselves. The study of law must, almost by definition, be broadened to include an understanding of its justification and effects.

In my view, economics comes at the top of any wider study of law for several straightforward reasons. First, it has a well-developed theory that is widely accepted by the economics profession. Most other social sciences cannot make this claim. Secondly, economics plays such an important part in the operation of the law that it would be foolhardy to ignore the subject. Laws impose and shift costs; they are costly, they create incentives and they alter behaviour. Thirdly, even if we do not accept that economic factors are important, we still need to know *how much* our preconceived ideas of rights, justice and morality are costing. Often the simple application of economics can reveal hidden and inconsistent assumptions and generate useful insights.

There is, however, no need to believe me. Let me call as my main witness one of the great legal minds of the common law, Mr Justice Oliver Wendell Holmes, and from what is reputed to be the 'most widely quoted legal article ever written'—'The Path of the Law'. Holmes, writing in 1897, looks forward to what he regards as the ideal state of legal education where the legal scholar's energy is directed to the

> 'study of the ends sought to be attained and the reasons for desiring them. As a step toward that ideal it seems to me that every lawyer ought to seek an understanding of economics. The present divorce between the schools of political economy and law seems to me evidence of how much progress in philosophical study still remains to be made. In . . . political economy . . . we are called on to consider and weigh the ends of legislation, the means of attaining them, and the cost. We learn that for everything we have to give up something else, and we are taught to set the advantage we gain against the other advantage we lose, and to know what we are doing when we elect'.[1]

[1] O. W. Holmes, 'The Path of the Law', *Harvard Law Review*, Vol. 10, 1897.

In short, lawyers should ask themselves whether the desired ends of laws 'are worth the price'. And, as Holmes emphasised, if the training of lawyers habitually led them to consider these questions in relation to a law, 'they sometimes would hesitate where they are now confident, and see that really they were taking sides upon debateable and often burning issues'. He concludes:

'... happiness, I am sure from having known many successful men, cannot be won simply by being counsel for great corporations and having an income of fifty thousand dollars. An intellect great enough to win the prize needs other food besides success. It is through [the study of the remoter and more general aspects of the law] ... that you not only become a great master in your calling, but connect your subject with the universe and catch an echo of the infinite, a glimpse of its unfathomable process, a hint of the universal law'.[1]

[1] *Ibid.*, p. 478.

QUESTIONS FOR DISCUSSION

1. Identify the differences between economic and legal reasoning.

2. Why is it that economics has been applied to the analysis of law and regulation?

3. Discuss the claim that lawyers are interested in justice, while economists are pre-occupied with economic efficiency.

4. What is the link between costs and benefits, on the one hand, and the way laws affect individual behaviour, on the other?

5. What is the Coase Theorem? Discuss its importance for the economic analysis of law.

6. Discuss the different theories of regulation.

7. Does the legal notion of 'reasonable care' have an economic definition?

8. Why do economists prefer fines as a criminal sanction?

9. What factors influence the extent and nature of plea bargains?

SELECT BIBLIOGRAPHY

Texts

Ackerman, B., *Reconstructuring American Law*, Cambridge, Mass.: Harvard University Press, 1984.

Barnes, D. W., *Statistics as Proof: Fundamentals of Quantitative Evidence*, Boston: Little Brown, 1983.

Bowles, R. A., *Law and the Economy*, Oxford: Martin Robertson, 1982.

Calabresi, G., *The Costs of Accidents – A Legal and Economic Analysis*, New Haven: Yale University Press, 1976.

Cooter, R., and Ulen, T., *Law and Economics*, Glenview, Ill.: Scott, Foresman, 1988.

Eggertsson, T., *Economic Behaviour and Institutions*, Cambridge: Cambridge University Press, 1990.

Goetz, C. J., *Law and Economics: Cases and Materials*, St. Paul, Minnesota: West, 1984.

Harris, D., *Remedies in Contract and Tort*, London: Weidenfeld and Nicolson, 1988.

Hirsch, W. A., *Law and Economics – An Introductory Analysis*, New York: Academic Press, 2nd edn., 1988.

Landes, W. M., and Posner, R. A., *The Economic Structure of Tort Law*, Cambridge, Mass.: Harvard University Press, 1987.

Mackaay, E., *Economics of Information and Law*, Boston: Kluwer Nijhoff, 1982.

Mercuro, N., and Ryan, T., *Law, Economics and Public Policy*, New York: JAI Press, 1984.

Murphy, J. G., and Coleman, J. L., *The Philosophy of Law*, Totowa, N.J.: Rowman and Allenheld, 1984.

Polinsky, A., *An Introduction to Law and Economics*, Boston: Little Brown, 2nd edn., 1989.

Posner, R. A., *Economic Analysis of Law*, Boston: Little Brown, 3rd edn., 1986.

——, *The Economics of Justice*, Cambridge, Mass.: Harvard University Press, 1981.

Shavell, S., *Economic Analysis of Accident Law*, Cambridge, Mass.: Harvard University Press, 1987.

Stephen, F. H., *The Economics of the Law*, Brighton: Harvester/Wheatsheaf Books, 1988.

Tullock, G., *The Logic of Law*, New York: Basic Books, 1970.

——, *Trials on Trials – The Pure Theory of Procedure*, New York: Columbia University Press, 1980.

Veljanovski, C. G., *The New Law-and-Economics – A Research Review*, Oxford: Centre for Socio-Legal Studies, 1982.

Anthologies

Ackerman, B. A. (ed.), *Economic Foundations of Property Law*, Boston: Little Brown, 1975.

Barzel, Y., *Economic Analysis of Property Rights*, Cambridge: Cambridge University Press, 1989.

Burrows, P., and Veljanovski, C. G. (eds.), *The Economic Approach to Law*, London: Butterworths, 1981.

Coase, R. H., *The Firm, the Market and the Law*, Chicago: Chicago University Press, 1988.

Cranston, R., and Schick, A. (eds.), *Law and Economics*, Canberra: Australian National University Press, 1982.

Dorn, J. A., and Manne, H. G. (eds.), *Economic Liberties and the Judiciary*, Fairfax: George Mason University Press, 1987.

Furbotn, E., and Pejovich, S. (eds.), *The Economics of Property Rights*, Cambridge, Mass.: Ballinger, 1974.

Goldberg, V. P. (ed.), *Readings in the Economics of Contract Law*, Cambridge: Cambridge University Press, 1989.

Kronman, A. T., and Posner, R. A. (eds.), *Economics of Contract*, Boston: Little Brown, 1979.

Kuperberg, M., and Beitz, C. (eds.), *Law, Economics and*

Philosophy—A Critical Introduction: with Applications to the Law of Torts, Totowa, N.J.: Rowman and Allenheld, 1983.

Manne, H. G. (ed.), *The Economics of Legal Relationships*, St. Paul, Minnesota: West, 1975.

Mercuro, N. (ed.), *Law and Economics*, Boston: Kluwer Nijhoff, 1988.

Ogus, A. I., and Veljanovski, C. G. (eds.), *Readings in the Economics of Law and Regulation*, Oxford: Oxford University Press, 1984.

Posner, R. A., *Tort—Cases and Economic Analysis*, Boston: Little Brown, 1982.

Rabin, R. L. (ed.), *Perspectives on Tort Law*, Boston: Little Brown, 1st edn., 1977; 2nd edn., 1983.

Rubin, P. H., *Business Firms and the Common Law: The Evolution of Efficient Rules*, New York: Praeger, 1983.

Skogh, G. (ed.), *Law and Economics*, Lund: Juridiska Foreningen i Lund, 1970.

Survey Articles/Symposia

Calabresi, G., *The New Economic Analysis of Law: Scholarship, Sophistry or Self-Indulgence?*, London: British Academy, 1981.

Cooter, R. D., 'Law and the Imperialism of Economics: An Introduction to the Economic Analysis of Law and a Review of the Major Books', *UCLA Law Review*, Vol. 29, 1982, pp. 1,260-69.

Cooter, R. D., and Rubinfeld, D. L., 'Economic Analysis of Legal Disputes and Their Resolution', *Journal of Economic Literature*, Vol. 27, 1988, pp. 1,067-97.

Kitch, E. W., 'The Fire of Truth: A Remembrance of Law and Economics at Chicago, 1932-1970', *Journal of Law and Economics*, Vol. 26, 1983, pp. 163-234.

Polinsky, A. M., 'Economic Analysis as a Potentially Defective Product: A Buyer's Guide to Posner's *Economic Analysis of Law*', *Harvard Law Review*, Vol. 87, 1974, pp. 1,655-81.

Posner, R. A., 'Some Uses and Abuses of Economics in Law', *University of Chicago Law Review*, Vol. 46, 1979, pp. 28-306.

Rowley, C. K., 'Social Sciences and the Law: The Relevance of Economic Theories', *Oxford Journal of Legal Studies*, Vol. 1, 1981, pp. 391-405.

Symposium: 'Change in the Common Law: Legal and Economic Perspectives', *Journal of Legal Studies*, Vol. 9, 1980, pp. 189-427.

Symposium: 'Symposium on Law and Economics', *Columbia Law Review*, Vol. 85, 1985, pp. 899-1,116.

Symposium: 'The Place of Economics in Legal Education', *Journal of Legal Education*, Vol. 33, 1983, pp. 183-376.

Symposium: 'Economists on the Bench', *Law and Contemporary Problems*, Vol. 50, 1987, pp. 1-286.

Veljanovski, C. G., 'The Economic Approach to Law—A Critical Introduction', *British Journal of Law and Society*, Vol. 7, 1980, pp. 158-93.

The Economics of Regulation

Bailey, E. E. (ed.), *Public Regulation: New Perspectives on Institutions and Policies*, Cambridge, Mass.: MIT Press, 1987.

Bebchuk, L. A., *The Law and Economics of Corporate Control*, Cambridge: Cambridge University Press, 1990.

Breyer, S., *Regulation and Its Reform*, Cambridge, Mass.: Harvard University Press, 1982.

Button, K., and Swann, D. (eds.), *The Age of Regulatory Reform*, Oxford: Clarendon Press, 1989.

Cowen, T. (ed.), *The Theory of Market Failure: A Critical Examination*, Fairfax, Virginia: George Mason University Press, 1988.

Fromm, G. (ed.), *Studies in Public Regulation*, Cambridge, Mass.: MIT Press, 1981.

Kahn, A. E., *The Economics of Regulation: Principles and Institutions*, Cambridge, Mass.: MIT Press, 1988.

Owen, B. M., and Braeutigan, R., *The Regulation Game: Strategic Use of the Administrative Process*, Cambridge, Mass.: Ballinger Publishing Company, 1978.

Peacock, A. (ed.), *The Regulation Game: How British and West German Companies Bargain with Government*, Oxford: Basil Blackwell, 1984.

Poole, R. W. Jr., *Instead of Regulation*, Lexington, Mass.: D.C. Heath, 1982.

Rowley, C. K., Tollison, R. D. and Tullock, G. (eds.), *The Political Economy of Rent-Seeking*, Boston: Kluwer Academic Publishers, 1988.

Utton, M. A., *The Economics of Regulating Industry*, Oxford: Basil Blackwell, 1986.

Waterson, M., *Regulation of the Firm and Natural Monopoly*, Oxford: Basil Blackwell, 1988.

<u>NEW TITLE</u>
Money, Credit and Inflation
GORDON PEPPER

When the Conservative Government took office in 1979, the principal economic objective was to bring down the rate of inflation. Historical evidence suggests that rising prices are associated by monetary growth being slightly faster than income growth.

In this *Research Monograph*, Gordon Pepper argues that the rate of inflation has not continued to fall but has risen and is currently one of the highest in the industrial world.

Monetarists have argued amongst themselves about the relative merits of broad money and narrow money, and the authorities have switched from one definition to another before abandoning all targets except that for M0. The story of the past decade is one of confusion, and this paper attempts to clarify the record. What were the signals coming from M0, the exchange rate and M4? Why was sterling pegged to the Deutschemark? What were the underlying causes of excessive monetary growth? Why was credit not controlled?

Gordon Pepper's answer is that the tools of monetary control were, and still are, inadequate. What he has done in this fascinating *Research Monograph* is to re-open the debate over monetary control which should have been addressed at the beginning of the 1980s.

The Author
Gordon Pepper is an Honorary Visiting Professor in the Department of Banking and Finance and Director of the Midland Montagu Centre for Financial Markets at the City University Business School. He is a Director and Senior Adviser of Midland Montagu, a Fellow of the Institute of Actuaries and a Fellow of the Society of Investment Analysts.

ISBN 0-255 36228-5   ***Research Monograph 44***   **£6.95**

THE INSTITUTE OF ECONOMIC AFFAIRS
2 Lord North Street, Westminster
London SW1P 3LB   Telephone: 071-799 3745